The Ultimate Deception
It Could Cost You Everything

Dear John and Kathy,
It was a wonderful blessing meeting both of you! Valerie and I wanted to thank you again for lending us your Oahu guide.
I hope this guide blesses your family as much as you have blessed us.

By
Stephen Gerard Michels
2013
Lamplighter Publishing

Steve

PROVERBS 1:7-9
JOHN 14:6

Available at www.amazon.com

1

The Ultimate Deception
It Could Cost You Everything

Dedication:

To Jesus, who loved me and gave His life for me. Worthy is the Lamb who was slain to receive power, and riches, and wisdom, and strength, and honor, and glory, and blessing.

To Tonya Jenkins, without whose encouragement this book would not have been written.

To my parents, Albert and Diane Michels, who's patience I sorely tried. Thank you, Mom and Dad for all that you sacrificed. Your legacy lives in the hearts of my children.

To my children, Matthew, Sarah, Michelle, Joshua, Jacob and Molly; you are my treasures. You know the right path. Follow Him.

To Cathy, Romans 8:38, 39

To all the sons and daughters who hunger and thirst for the truth.

A special thanks to my daughter Sarah for the artwork.

Acknowledgements:

Dietrich Bonheoffer, Oswald Chambers, Greg Dimeolo, John Foxe, Andrew Murray, Donald Stamps, Todd Tomasella, R.A. Torrey

The Ultimate Deception
It Could Cost You Everything

The purpose of this book is to:

- Present the Truth
- Reconcile lost souls to a Holy God
- Warn the disobedient to repent
- Be a watchman for the saved
- Exhort the body of Christ (believers) unto good works
- Teach believers the importance of obeying the commands of Jesus
- Advance the kingdom of God

Note to Reader regarding Bible quotes:

- All Scripture references are from the King James Version
- Underlines added by the author for emphasis
- Words not in bold (in parenthesis) are the author's

4

Dear reader,

The message you are about to read in this book was heard by the citizens of the city of Berea in approximately 63 A.D.

After hearing it, this is what they did:

...they <u>received the word with all readiness of mind</u>, and <u>searched the scriptures daily</u>, whether those things were so. Therefore <u>many of them believed</u>; also of honourable women which were Greeks, and of men, not a few. Acts 17:11-12

It is my greatest desire in writing this book that you too will search the Bible to see whether or not the words you read in the following pages are true. I encourage you to have your Bible open as you read this message and I prayerfully hope you will take the time to refer to the Scriptures noted. You have everything to gain if you do and everything to lose if you don't.

Be a Berean.

Yours in Christ,
Stephen Michels

Forward

This is a dangerous book. It is sure to eradicate lies, false notions and deception, as well as false religious beliefs and philosophies (Colossians 2:8). Read this book to be wise, discerning, and a disciple of Jesus.

The author of this book, "The Ultimate Deception", sets forth the clear message of the Original Gospel while dispelling the epidemic of lies permeating the misguided thoughts of the majority of those who claim to be following Christ.

I recommend this volume to every person who names the name of Jesus Christ. Stephen Michels helps the disciple to find refuge in divine truth, as he rightly divides the Word of God and exposes the many strands of error sown through deceitful religious lies by the enemy of all souls.

This book is packed with vital information on all the most prevalent antichrist cults and provides an overview of the errors that they promulgate. After reading this powerful book, the disciple will be equipped to continue to grow in the grace of Christ and discern all that opposes our wonderful, nail-scarred, soon to be returning Lord and Savior!

Todd Tomasella
www.safeguardyoursoul.com

Contents

Introduction

Pilate therefore said unto him, Art thou a king then? Jesus answered, Thou sayest that I am a king. To this end was I born, and for this cause came I into the world, that I should bear witness unto the truth. Every one that is of the truth heareth my voice. Pilate saith unto him, What is truth? And when he had said this, he went out again unto the Jews, and saith unto them, I find in him no fault at all. John 18:37-38

Today, among the many cultures of our world, there exists a plethora of doctrines, philosophies, religions and ideas regarding spiritual truth. The men and women responsible for these many and varied ideas include a number of well known (and some not so well known), self-proclaimed prophets, visionaries, spiritual leaders, and philosophers. These individuals have infused their own personal set of principles and beliefs into the hearts and minds of vast numbers of men and women over the course of history. The staggering number of souls who adhere to such diverse teachings is a testimony to the success of these belief systems. The true source inspiring these doctrines remains hidden to most.

How is one to know the truth? Is it possible to identify spiritual truth from error? Does truth exist and, if it does, which set of beliefs or doctrines are true and which are false? Is this information important to know? Is it even relevant in our modern society? Should we seek after the truth? If so, why should we?

Dear reader, I submit to you that spiritual truth can be known and that discerning correct doctrine is of the utmost importance to every living soul. There can be no knowledge more important or more needful for all humankind than to know the truth. Please join me as we explore this concept in the following pages.

My purpose in writing this book is to present the unequivocal truth to those who are earnestly seeking an answer to the most important question of life that one may ask. That is, what is "Truth" and can it be known with certainty? Can we know and be sure of our eternal destiny and what is required of us (if anything) in this short life? Is it possible for us to be deceived and make fatal mistakes regarding our future; mistakes that will cost us our very souls? How do we recognize truth from error when confronted by so many conflicting opinions from numerous so-called "Christian" and/or "Spiritual" leaders? What is the most precious possession we have and can it be stolen from us unawares? Are there dangerous enemies out there, posing as friends, who will lead us into the fire? One day, will it be too late? Have we been deceived?

If, in your heart, you sense that all is not right in these turbulent days and that something is missing, then this book is for you. If you are truly hungering and searching for righteousness, then please read the message this book contains and take time to consider it thoughtfully. Before you do, ask God to open the eyes of your heart and to give you understanding. If you have never prayed before, go to a quiet place alone and ask God to reveal the truth to you. Challenge Him to make himself known to your heart. Make certain that you confirm what you read and hear with what is written in an Authorized Version of the Holy Bible (all quotes for this book are taken from the King James Version). If you are concerned about others being deceived, get this book into their hands.

I believe with all my heart that the truth, which can be known, has been questioned, perverted, diluted, sabotaged, and outright denied. I believe that there are many, many souls in a place right now who would give anything and everything to have another opportunity to know the truth before it was too late for them. Of all the deceptions found in our world today, spiritual deception and self-deception are by far the most deadly. These deceptions could cost you everything before you even realize it and, when you do, it will be too late.

My prayer for you, dear reader, is that God will grant you ears to hear while there is still time. Do not wait. There are no guarantees that any of us will be here tomorrow.

Chapter 1

RELIGION VERSUS RELATIONSHIP

And ye shall know the truth, and the truth shall make you free.
John 8:32

Many have heard the inspiring words written above and yet do not know who spoke them. Nor are they aware that the speaker of these words had more to say within the context of this quote. I don't know about you but, as far as I am concerned, I certainly do not want anyone editing out any information available that may be very relevant to such an important topic as "The Truth."

Dear reader and living soul most precious in the eyes of God, it is my heart's urgent desire that you come to know the truth. In a world full of deception, corruption and moral decay, I want to comfort you with the understanding that truth does exist and that it is not far from any of us. In our culture today, the prevalent ideology expressed by most holding the microphone is that there are no moral absolutes, no right or wrong way, and thus no real truth.

What we are left with by those who claim to be wise and what we are supposed to blindly accept is the concept of "Situational Ethics." Well, what is that? In essence, situational ethics is a code of behavior that evaluates acts in light of their situational context rather than by the application of moral absolutes. In other words, if you believe in your own wisdom that your behavior is justifiable considering the circumstances of your life at the time, then it is moral, ethical and right behavior. Now I ask you to please consider the thought that, if we are honest with ourselves, it is not difficult to see the fatal flaw with this philosophy and the obvious catastrophic consequences that will be the result of such thinking. Let me translate for you the true meaning of situational ethics so that there will be no misunderstanding. If you choose to live your life by this philosophy, then you are telling the world that you are your own god. Whether you realize it or not, this is the result of your decision; despite your intentions. You are living your life with yourself in the center of the circle. You have made the choice to interact with everyone and everything else solely on the basis of how it affects you.

With the understanding we now have regarding this philosophy, it becomes readily apparent that this way of thinking would be easily accepted by most, as it allows each of us to construct our own personal set of beliefs and doctrines or adhere to whatever "Religion" suits us. As far as the majority is concerned, if you don't like one you see go ahead and make up your own. "Just don't infringe on my way of life or beliefs" seems to be the common opinion and popular way today. While following this philosophy for living one's life may appear wise and tolerant on the surface, the reality is something else altogether. Indeed, it seems to be a very good ideology for us to think that all roads lead to Heaven. However, we must remember that we are not the Creator. Rather, we are the created ones.

There is a way that seemeth right unto a man, but the end thereof are the ways of death. Proverbs 16:25

The resulting fruit of this "Wisdom of men" is plainly observable in our world. We see it manifested in the cornucopia of religions and doctrines of our day. For example, here is a sampling of religions and doctrines which hold the belief that there is no hell:

Buddhism, Confucianism, Hare Krishna, Hinduism, Black Islam, Jainism, Rastafarianism, Gypsies, Shinto, Sikhism, Taoism, Agnosticism, Atheism, Marxism, Naturalism, Secular Humanism, Necromancy, Rosicrucian's, Wicca, Christian Science, New Age, Scientology, Theosophy, Transcendental Meditation, Unitarian Universalist, The Way International, et al.

Does the degree of popularity of a particular doctrine make it true? Is the fact that we are attracted to what we hear, make what we hear factual and true? It never ceases to amaze me that many organized religions acknowledge and affirm that Jesus was a great teacher and prophet, while at the same time denying the truth of the things he taught and prophesied about! To hold such a position is dangerously deceptive, doctrinally dishonest, and nothing more than blatant hypocrisy. This is very hazardous ground to be standing on as we consider the supreme importance of truth, the critical need to know it, and what the very serious consequences of not knowing it will be for each one of us.

What did Jesus teach us about hell?

And fear not them which kill the body, but are not able to kill the soul: but rather <u>fear him which is able to destroy both soul and body in hell</u>. Matthew 10:28

There was a certain rich man, which was clothed in purple and fine linen, and fared sumptuously every day: And there was a certain beggar named Lazarus, which was laid at his gate, full of sores, And desiring to be fed with the crumbs which fell from the rich man's table: moreover the dogs came and licked his sores. And it came to pass, that the beggar died, and was carried by the angels into Abraham's bosom: the rich man also died, and was buried; <u>And in hell he lift up his eyes, being in torments</u>, and seeth Abraham afar off, and Lazarus in his

bosom. And he cried and said, Father Abraham, have mercy on me, and send Lazarus, that he may dip the tip of his finger in water, and cool my tongue; <u>for I am tormented in this flame</u>. But Abraham said, Son, remember that thou in thy lifetime receivedst thy good things, and likewise Lazarus evil things: but now he is comforted, and thou art tormented. And beside all this, between us and you there is a great gulf fixed: so that they which would pass from hence to you cannot; neither can they pass to us, that would come from thence. Then he said, I pray thee therefore, father, that thou wouldest send him to my father's house: <u>For I have five brethren; that he may testify unto them, lest they also come into this place of torment</u>. Abraham saith unto him, They have Moses and the prophets; let them hear them. And he said, Nay, father Abraham: but if one went unto them from the dead, they will repent. And he said unto him, If they hear not Moses and the prophets, neither will they be persuaded, though one rose from the dead. Luke 16:19-31

And if thy hand offend thee, cut it off: it is better for thee to enter into life maimed, than having two hands <u>to go into hell, into the fire that never shall be quenched</u>: Where their worm dieth not, <u>and the fire is not quenched</u>. And if thy foot offend thee, cut it off: it is better for thee to enter halt into life, than having two feet <u>to be cast into hell, into the fire that never shall be quenched</u>: Where their worm dieth not, <u>and the fire is not quenched</u>. And if thine eye offend thee, pluck it out: it is better for thee to enter into the kingdom of God with one eye, than having two eyes <u>to be cast into hell fire</u>: Where their worm dieth not, <u>and the fire is not quenched</u>. Mark 9:43-48

Many religious organizations go even further in that they doctrinally deny that Jesus is the Son of God. By promulgating such a belief, they grant unto themselves a very useful tool for

14

dismissing any of His teachings. Below is a very incomplete list of those organizations which do not believe that Jesus is the Son of God:

ANTHROPOSOPHICAL SOCIETY – Jesus was just a man until age 30 and then he received "Christ Essence."

ASSEMBLIES OF YAHWEH – Denies the Trinity.

ASTARA – Teaches a "Cosmic Christ", denies the eternal nature of Jesus.

THE BAHA'I FAITH – Christ is only one of the nine great manifestations of divinity. Baha'u'llah, the founder, is greater.

BLACK MUSLIM – Jesus was black and only a prophet.

BRANHAMISM – Jesus was created and is not eternal, denies the Trinity.

BUDDHISM – Christ is not recognized as Deity. Zen Buddhism also does not affirm the existence of the living God.

CABALA (KABBALAH) – Recognizes only two deities: the hidden god, the infinite great divine Nothing and the dynamic god of religious experience, mystical.

CENTER FOR SPIRITUAL AWARENESS – Jesus was a man who reached "Christ consciousness."

CHRISTADELPHIANS – Jesus did not exist before birth to Mary. He is not God.

CHRISTIAN SCIENCE – Christ is a Divine Idea, His blood doesn't cleanse us.

CHURCH OF GOD INTERNATIONAL – God is a family, Christ is the only human saved so far, denies the Trinity.

CHURCH OF THE LIVING WORD (THE WALK) – Followers become the Living Word (Christ) to the world.

CHURCH UNIVERSAL AND TRIUMPHANT (SUMMIT INTERNATIONAL/ SUMMIT LIGHTHOUSE) – Jesus was a man with "Christ consciousness."

DAWN BIBLE STUDENTS ASSOCIATION – Jesus was created and is not God, denies the Trinity.

ECKANKAR (THE ANCIENT ART OF SOUL TRAVEL) – Christ is god as all men are god.

EMISSARIES OF DIVINE LIGHT (ONTOLOGISTS) – Do not accept the atoning work of Christ, mystical.

ESALEN INSTITUTE – "Human Potential" movement, mystical.

EST (ERHARD SEMINAR TRAININGS) (THE FORUM) – Each person is a god himself.

ETERNAL FLAME – Charles Paul Brown, the leader, claims to be the very body and blood of Christ.

THE FOUNDATION FAITH OF THE MILLENNIUM – Denies the deity of Christ, He was only a prophet.

FOUNDATION OF HUMAN UNDERSTANDING – Neglects Christ or mentions him in a negative context.

FREEMASONRY – Jesus was a man like us.

GLOBAL CHURCH OF GOD – Denies the Trinity, God is a Family.

HARE KRISHNA – Jesus is one of their gurus, but Hare Krishna is their god.

HINDUISM – There is no need for a personal savior. Each one becomes a god or attains "Cosmic consciousness."

"I AM" MOVEMENT – Jesus is one of many ascended masters.

INNER PEACE MOVEMENT – Jesus was a man who reached "Christ consciousness." God is impersonal.

ISLAM – Teaches that God (Allah) has no son in direct opposition to the Bible. Jesus was only a prophet of Allah, superseded by Mohammed.

JAINISM – Denies the existence of a Creator, Humanists.

JEHOVAH'S WITNESSES (THE WATCHTOWER BIBLE & TRACT SOCIETY) – Jesus was created as Archangel Michael, a lesser god and became only a good man. He died, ceased to exist, and was re-created as Michael again in heaven, He is not God, denies the Trinity.

LIFESPRING – Similar to EST, each person is a god.

MOONIES (THE UNIFICATION CHURCH) – Christ failed in His earthly mission leaving Reverend Moon to finish the task, believe Moon to be "Lord of the Second Advent."

MORMONS (THE CHURCH OF JESUS CHRIST OF LATTER-DAY SAINTS) – Jesus was born in heaven as the spirit child of Elohim (Heavenly Father) by one of his wives, and Jesus' brother is Lucifer, who became Satan. Jesus is one of many gods.

NEO-GNOSTICISM – Jesus one who possessed a "Higher consciousness." He did not die for man's sins.

NEW AGE MOVEMENT – Promises to produce the "Messiah" out of a coalition of cult/occult groups. Jesus was only a great teacher.

PEOPLES TEMPLE CHRISTIAN CHURCH – Jim Jones considered himself the reincarnation of Jesus Christ and led over 900 followers to their deaths.

PHILADELPHIA CHURCH OF GOD – Denies the Trinity. God is a family.

PROCESS CHURCH OF THE FINAL JUDGEMENT – Jesus was a man.

RAJNEESH MEDITATION CENTERS – God is not a person. Existence is without cause.

ROMAN CATHOLICISM – A works based religion, denies the efficacy, uniqueness and exclusivity of salvation by grace alone, through faith in Jesus; teach a myriad of false doctrines, including Mary/Pope worship, Peter as the Rock, Purgatory, infant baptism.

ROSICRUCIANISM - Reincarnated man is a manifestation of the "Cosmic Christ."

SCIENTOLOGY – All are gods including Christ.

SEVENTH-DAY ADVENTISM – Jesus is God but also he is the archangel Michael. Christ did not complete atonement at Calvary.

SIKHISM – If a person works his way to salvation, he is absorbed into the formless God.

SILVA MIND CONTROL – Seek oneness with pantheistic deity; teaches "Christ awareness."

SWEDENBORGISM – Calls Jesus God but denies the personality of the Holy Spirit.

TAOISM – Worships creator principle of the Tao or "The Force", ignores Christ.

THEOSOPHY – Christ is the reincarnation of the world's soul.

T.M. (TRANSCENDENTAL MEDITATION) – Christ is a prophet. Mankind can meditate into "God awareness" without a mediator.

UNITARIANS (UNITARIAN UNIVERSALIST ASSOCIATION) – Jesus was an extraordinarily good man only.

UNITED PENTECOSTAL CHURCH – Denies the Trinity.

THE WAY INTERNATIONAL – Jesus is not God.

YOGA – A series of exercises designed to align your body to absorb the "Cosmic Force", an impersonal deity.

ZOROASTRIANISM – Does not recognize a personal God.

Did you observe a repetitive pattern in the preceding list?

Note the staggering number of individuals who adhere to the following major religions existing in the world today:

Islam: 1.5 billion

Roman Catholicism: 1.2 billion

Secular/Nonreligious/Agnostic/Atheist: 1.1 billion

Hinduism: 900 million

Chinese traditional religion: 394 million

Buddhism: 376 million

Primal-Indigenous: 300 million

African Traditional: 100 million

Sikhism: 23 million

Spiritism: 15 million

Judaism: 14 million

Baha'i: 7 million

Jainism: 4.2 million

Shinto: 4 million

Zoroastrianism: 2.6 million

Neo-Paganism: 1 million

Unitarian-Universalism: 800 thousand

Rastafarianism: 600 thousand

Scientology: 500 thousand

This then, is the manifestation of man's wisdom. We are left with an incredibly tangled mixture of confusing and conflicting doctrines which have the effect of bringing even the most tenacious seeker of truth to despair. Considering the fact that situational ethics is so widespread in our world today, one must consider the source of such a popular doctrine. Where did it come from? Why is it so accepted by the majority in our world? We need look no further than the written Word of God for the answer.

How art thou fallen from heaven, O Lucifer, son of the morning! how art thou cut down to the ground, which didst weaken the nations! For thou hast said in thine heart, I will ascend into heaven, I will exalt my throne above the stars of God: I will sit also upon the mount of the congregation, in the sides of the north: I will ascend above the heights of the clouds; I will be like the most High. Isaiah 14:12-14

The truth is that none other than Satan, the fallen arch angel Lucifer, is the spiritual source behind these soul-damning doctrines. He has very successfully infused his deception into the hearts of mankind ever since the fall of Adam and Eve. He has always wanted to be his own god and be worshipped by man as such. He rebelled against his maker who is God and, through pride, fell by his own transgression. Tragically, he has found a number of powerful ways to influence mankind after his own heart; false religion, vain philosophy, and the pursuit of temporal gain such as money, possessions, and power. He tempts mankind through the lust of the eyes, the lust of the flesh, and the pride of life. He is the father of lies and of the children of disobedience. His ultimate goal is the destruction of as many souls as possible in the fires of hell.

Jesus very clearly told us:

I am the way, the truth, and the life: no man cometh unto the Father, but by me. John 14:6

Jesus very clearly warned us:

Enter ye in at the strait gate: for wide is the gate, and broad is the way, that leadeth to destruction, and many there be which go in thereat: Because strait is the gate, and narrow is the way, which leadeth unto life, and few there be that find it. Matthew 7:13-14

Many today are very comfortable in their religion and believe it to be a legitimate way for them to live their lives. The prevalent thinking seems to be, "Whatever rules you have committed yourself to, just follow them to the best of your ability and that will suffice." "Religion" has been a very successful tool in Satan's arsenal and has had the devastating effect of deceiving many souls. Its' use continues to play a major role in accomplishing the desires of the arch enemy of God; the perversion of the truth and the destruction of mankind. Please read the following words of Jesus very carefully:

Not every one that saith unto me, Lord, Lord, shall enter into the kingdom of heaven; but he that doeth the will of my Father which is in heaven. Many will say to me in that day, Lord, Lord, have we not prophesied in thy name? and in thy name have cast out devils? and in thy name done many wonderful works? And then will I profess unto them, I never knew you: depart from me, ye that work iniquity. Matthew 7:21-23

Did you catch that? Many will try to enter the kingdom of heaven on the basis of their own personal "Religion." In other words, many believe that the path they have chosen for themselves and the beliefs which they have dedicated themselves to will satisfy God. They will say that they have done many wonderful and good works on behalf of Jesus. He will tell them to go depart from Him because He never knew them!

Is there a road we should be walking on? How do we find it?

Trust in the LORD with all thine heart; and <u>lean not unto thine own understanding</u>. <u>In all thy ways acknowledge him</u>, and <u>he shall direct thy paths</u>. <u>Be not wise in thine own eyes</u>: <u>fear the LORD, and depart from evil</u>. Proverbs 3:5-7

Please take a moment to meditate on the above Scripture. There is <u>much truth</u> in these words.

Now, let us revisit the Scripture quoted at the beginning of this chapter:

And ye shall know the truth, and the truth shall make you free. John 8:32

Who spoke those words and did the speaker have more to say?

Here is the quote in context:

Then said Jesus to those Jews which believed on him, <u>If ye continue in my word</u>, then are ye my disciples indeed; And ye shall know the truth, and the truth shall make you free. John 8:31-32

We now have the understanding that truth can be known and what is required for it to be known. We also know who has the truth and what knowing the truth will do for us. This is incredibly good news for all of us. This is the Gospel of Jesus Christ. When we

23

find Jesus, we find the truth. <u>Jesus is the truth</u>. Knowing Jesus, believing on Him, and continuing in His word means that we know what He said, we believe what He said, and we obey what He said.

Knowing what we just learned, it is now readily apparent that if we do not know Jesus, we MUST do whatever is required in order to find Him and invite Him into our lives.

The apostle Paul was radically changed after meeting Jesus (more on that in a later chapter). As a matter of fact, Paul suddenly found out that the "Religion" he previously believed in and the doctrines that he had so zealously followed all his life were unacceptable to God. He had some critical and life-changing truths to impart to a group of fellow believers regarding who Jesus is and what it means to know Him. He wrote to the Christians at Colosse testifying to the truth of Jesus, and what knowing Him means for all of us. With these words, we learn the truth as to who Jesus is, the truth about our purpose in God's plans and the truth about what is required of us to fulfill God's will for our lives acceptably.

In the first chapter of Colossians, Paul writes:

Paul, an apostle of Jesus Christ <u>by the will of God</u>, and Timotheus our brother,

Paul was called by God's will to be His apostle to the gentiles.

To the saints and faithful brethren in Christ which are at Colosse: Grace be unto you, and peace, from God our Father and the Lord Jesus Christ.

We give thanks to God and <u>the Father of our Lord Jesus Christ</u>, praying always for you,

Jesus is the Son of God.

Since we heard of your <u>faith in Christ Jesus</u>, and of <u>the love</u> which ye have to all the saints,

The most important fruit that manifests in our lives after meeting Jesus is <u>love toward others</u>.

For <u>the hope which is laid up for you in heaven</u>, whereof ye heard before in the <u>word of the truth of the gospel</u>;

The truth of the Gospel, which means "Good news", will impart hope into the hearer's heart.

Which is come unto you, as it is in all the world; and <u>bringeth forth fruit, as it doth also in you, since the day ye heard of it, and knew the grace of God in truth</u>:

As ye also learned of Epaphras our dear fellowservant, who is for you a faithful minister of Christ;

Who also declared unto us your love in the Spirit.

For this cause we also, since the day we heard it, do not cease to pray for you, and to desire that <u>ye might be filled with the knowledge of his will in all wisdom and spiritual understanding</u>;

Jesus is the fullness of the wisdom of God.

That <u>ye might walk worthy of the Lord unto all pleasing, being fruitful in every good work, and increasing in the knowledge of God</u>;

We are to be actively fruitful in demonstrating our faith by our good works, as well as seeking an ever more intimate relationship with Jesus and the Father.

Strengthened with all might, according to <u>his glorious power</u>, unto all <u>patience</u> and <u>longsuffering</u> with <u>joyfulness</u>;

We will be well equipped with His power in us to be patient and we will be filled with joy as we walk with Him.

<u>Giving thanks unto the Father</u>, which hath made us meet (fit) **<u>to be partakers of the inheritance of the saints in light</u>:**

Through the sacrifice of Jesus, we have been adopted into the family of God.

Who hath <u>delivered us from the power of darkness</u>, and hath <u>translated us into the kingdom of his dear Son</u>:

<u>In whom we have redemption through his blood, even the forgiveness of sins</u>:

This is the good news! Jesus, the Son of God, paid the price for our sins!

<u>Who is the image of the invisible God</u>, the firstborn of every creature:

If you want to see God, look at His Son - Jesus.

For <u>by him</u> were all things created, that are in heaven, and that are in earth, visible and invisible, whether they be thrones, or dominions, or principalities, or powers: <u>all things were created by him, and for him</u>:

This is who Jesus is!

And <u>he is before all things, and by him all things consist.</u>

This is who Jesus is!

And **he is the head of the body, the church**: **who is the beginning, the firstborn from the dead; that in all things he might have the preeminence.**

This is who Jesus is!

For it pleased the Father that in him should all fulness dwell;

This is who Jesus is!

And, having made peace through the blood of his cross, by him to reconcile all things unto himself; by him, I say, whether they be things in earth, or things in heaven.

We can have peace with God through His Son, Jesus.

And you, that were sometime alienated and enemies in your mind by wicked works, yet now hath he reconciled In the body of his flesh through death, to present you holy and unblameable and unreproveable in his sight:

Jesus's death gives us life!

If ye continue in the faith grounded and settled, and be not moved away from the hope of the gospel, which ye have heard, and which was preached to every creature which is under heaven; whereof I Paul am made a minister;

Only a living faith will save any of us. We must always examine ourselves to see if we are continuing in the faith. Our salvation depends upon it and our relationship with Jesus will assure our hearts.

Who now rejoice in my sufferings for you, and fill up that which is behind of the afflictions of Christ in my flesh for his body's sake, which is the church:

Whereof I am made a minister, according to the dispensation of God which is given to me for you, to fulfil the word of God;

Even <u>the mystery which hath been hid from ages and from generations, but now is made manifest to his saints</u>:

To whom God would make known what is the riches of the glory of this mystery among the Gentiles; <u>which is Christ in you, the hope of glory</u>:

What is the mystery? Everyone may be reconciled to God through the sacrifice of Jesus.

Whom we preach, <u>warning every man</u>, and <u>teaching every man in all wisdom</u>; that we may present every man <u>perfect in Christ Jesus</u>: Whereunto I also labour, striving according to <u>his working</u>, which <u>worketh in me mightily</u>. Colossians 1

James, the leader of the Jerusalem church tells us very clearly what freedom in Christ is.

Wherefore lay apart all filthiness and superfluity of naughtiness, and receive with meekness the engrafted word, which is able to save your souls. But <u>be ye doers of the word</u>, and not hearers only, deceiving your own selves. For if any be a hearer of the word, and not a doer, he is like unto a man beholding his natural face in a glass: For he beholdeth himself, and goeth his way, and straightway forgetteth what manner of man he was. But <u>whoso looketh into the perfect law of liberty, and continueth therein, he being not a forgetful hearer, but a</u>

doer of the work, this man shall be blessed in his deed. James 1:21-25

Dear reader, this is the truth. If you are sincerely hungering after the truth, you will eventually come to the end of yourself. If you humble yourself and cry out to God, you will find Him and you will receive the greatest gift you could ever be given; the gift of eternal life through His Son. When you meet Jesus and begin a relationship with Him, you will learn that He loves you more than you are able to comprehend. You will fall ever more deeply in love with Him as you grow in your relationship with Him and realize the price He paid for your life. If you allow Him to enter into your heart, repent and believe the good news, then He will become your first love for the rest of your life!

If you have never prayed before, please take the time to find a quiet place and speak these words out loud:

Oh God, I know that I have been living my life on my own terms. I have put myself first in all my plans and have not found peace. I want to know You and I want to know the truth. I believe that Jesus died for my sins. I am so sorry for the wrong that I have done and I want to change my ways and the road I am on. Please come into my heart Jesus and make me a new creation. I surrender my life to You and ask You to by my Lord and Savior. Amen.

Chapter 2

THE SPIRIT OF TRUTH VERSUS THE SPIRIT OF ERROR

Beloved, believe not every spirit, but try the spirits whether they are of God: because many false prophets are gone out into the world. 1 John 4:1

In the previous chapter, we discovered that there are many diverse religions, doctrines and philosophies in our world; all with conflicting and contradicting claims to the truth. The inspiration for these doctrines is nothing less than the spirit of error.

Even within the realm of professing Christianity, the spirit of error manifests itself in many deceitful ways. Over time, cardinal doctrines of the faith have been distorted, perverted and even discarded with tragic consequences for many souls. When any individual does not take the written Word of God, as well as his or her relationship with Jesus seriously, he or she becomes highly susceptible to deception and deadly doctrinal errors that can destroy the most precious thing that one has; his or her own soul. Popular doctrines of our day that have been inspired by the spirit of error include: the highly dangerous doctrine that one cannot lose his or her salvation (known as "Once Saved Always Saved" or OSAS), reincarnation (in all its' variations, including purgatory), Gnostic and Calvinistic doctrines which do not require obedience to the faith, and the revolting prosperity gospel propagated by legions of modern day hucksters.

What is the spirit of error? Let us examine the origins of this deadly, deceiving spirit. In doing so, we will discover the source and pattern for all false teaching.

What follows is a conversation I had not too long ago with a woman who was raised Catholic, but had indicated that she was now "Spiritual". We were enjoying casual conversation when she suddenly asked me, "What is your passion?" Without even thinking about it, I responded, "God". She then launched into a lengthy monologue about how she wasn't sure if she believed in reincarnation, but she believed that we are all on a spiritual journey and she didn't believe there is a God up there, but that god is in all of us and we each have our own truth, and we are all children of God, and people are basically good, etc., etc.

As I listened to her, Scripture after Scripture came into my mind which directly refuted every assertion she was making and every declaration she was so certain of. After waiting for her to finish, I started referring to the Holy Bible, the written Word of God. My purpose was to explain to her that all "Religion" is founded on the idea that we are all gods and/or can become gods by our own good works, wisdom, or effort, and that this is what the arch enemy of God wants us to think. It all started in the Garden of Eden, when man fell through the deception of Satan.

God:

But of the tree of the knowledge of good and evil, thou shalt not eat of it: for in the day that thou eatest thereof <u>thou shalt surely die</u>. Genesis 2:17

Satan:

And the serpent said unto the woman, <u>Ye shall not surely die</u>: For God doth know that in the day ye eat thereof, then your eyes shall be opened, and <u>ye shall be as gods</u>, knowing good and evil. Genesis 3: 4, 5

Tragically, Eve did not recognize that Satan promised what she already had and ended up stealing it from her. She and Adam were already walking intimately with the one true God! They needed nothing! The "Knowledge" that she and Adam gained is the same "Knowledge" that Satan still grants today to all that follow him; it is the knowledge of evil, which is the knowledge of SIN! Remember beloved, Satan is a master deceiver, the father of lies, and a murderer. He creates nothing and seeks only to destroy.

Now, let us return to my conversation with the woman. By saying that she was "Spiritual", I informed her that she was only reaffirming the same old "many spokes in the wheel" philosophy of the spirit of error that is deceptively manifesting itself today through ecumenism/universalism. This is the idea that all paths lead to heaven and it is rampant in our world today. I responded with Scriptures which state who God is, who we are, who Jesus is, and why He came here. I didn't get very far and when I rebutted her contention that people are all basically good with the following Scripture,

The heart is <u>deceitful</u> above all things, and <u>desperately wicked</u>: who can know it? Jeremiah 17:9,

she actually put her hands over her ears and told me to stop and that this sounded like preaching. She said she was getting a bad feeling and didn't want to talk about it anymore. She declared that we were obviously in total disagreement. Having been raised Catholic as well, I knew that she had NO IDEA what I was talking about because she was never exposed to or taught the truth contained in God's written Word. Her response was not surprising as it is one of only two responses given whenever the truth is spoken. Why?

For the word of God is quick, and powerful, and sharper than any twoedged sword, piercing even to the dividing asunder of soul and spirit, and of the joints and marrow, and <u>is a discerner of the thoughts and intents of the heart</u>. Hebrews 4:12

This whole exchange left my heart very troubled for this deceived soul. The next morning, as I was starting my Bible reading, the Holy Spirit comforted me with the following Scriptures which directly refuted this woman's main contention, as she stated in her own words, "There is no God up there." It is recorded in the Scriptures that King Nebuchadnezzar had a dream which none of his wise men, astrologers, sorcerers or magicians could interpret. So, he sent out a decree ordering that they all be executed. Daniel, having heard this, prayed for understanding and this is the result:

Daniel answered in the presence of the king, and said, The secret which the king hath demanded cannot the wise men, the astrologers, the magicians, the soothsayers, shew unto the king; But <u>there is a God in heaven</u> that revealeth secrets, and maketh known to the king Nebuchadnezzar what shall be in the latter days. Thy dream, and the visions of thy head upon thy bed, are these; As for thee, O king, thy thoughts came into thy mind upon thy bed, what should come to pass hereafter: and he that revealeth secrets maketh known to thee what shall come to pass. Daniel 2:27-29

THERE IS A GOD IN HEAVEN!

Dear reader, as you are learning about the truth, you will encounter many who are influenced by the spirit of error. They will say they are "Spiritual". Well, Satan is spiritual. The fallen angels are spiritual. Demons are spiritual. The countless number of lost souls in hell are spiritual. If all a person can tell you about what they believe is that they are spiritual, then let me interpret for you what that means. It means that they are:

Foolish

The fool hath said in his heart, There is no God. Psalm 14:1

Deceived

Yea, and all that will live godly in Christ Jesus shall suffer persecution. But evil men and seducers shall wax worse and worse, deceiving, and being deceived. 2 Timothy 3:12, 13

Disobedient

Wherein in time past ye walked according to the course of this world, according to the prince of the power of the air, the spirit that now worketh in the children of disobedience: Ephesians 2:2

Children of the devil

Ye are of your father the devil, and the lusts of your father ye will do. He was a murderer from the beginning, and abode not in the truth, because there is no truth in him. When he speaketh a lie, he speaketh of his own: for he is a liar, and the father of it. John 8:44

Under the wrath of God

34

For the <u>wrath of God</u> is revealed from heaven against all ungodliness and unrighteousness of men, who hold the truth in unrighteousness; Because that which may be known of God is manifest in them; for God hath shewed it unto them. Romans 1:18, 19

<u>Damned unless they repent</u>

For the mystery of iniquity doth already work: only he who now letteth will let, until he be taken out of the way. And then shall that Wicked be revealed, whom the Lord shall consume with the spirit of his mouth, and shall destroy with the brightness of his coming: Even him, whose coming is after the working of Satan with all power and signs and lying wonders, And <u>with all deceivableness of unrighteousness in them that perish; because they received not the love of the truth, that they might be saved</u>. And for this cause God shall send them strong delusion, that they should believe a lie: 2 Thessalonians 2:7-11

Dear reader, I urge you to please re-read the preceding quote. God shall the send the lost a <u>strong delusion</u>, that they should believe a lie!

Why?

<u>Because they received not the truth</u>!

Why?

He that believeth on him is not condemned: but <u>he that believeth not is condemned already, because he hath not believed in the name of the only begotten Son of God</u>. And this is the condemnation, that light is come into the world, and <u>men</u>

35

loved darkness rather than light, because their deeds were evil. For every one that doeth evil hateth the light, neither cometh to the light, lest his deeds should be reproved. John 3:18-20

This should make every living soul tremble and fall on his or her knees, crying out to God that they would NOT be deceived!

So, we are back to the foundational concept of truth versus error. It greatly saddens my heart to hear people tell me, "You have your truth and I have mine." Truth is not relative. It is not subjective. It is not variable or dependent on the ever shifting sands of situational ethics or "Politically correct" public opinion so commonly observed in society today. We have been given many, many great and precious promises by God, as well warnings for disobedience. Every one of those promises was, is, and will be fulfilled in the person of Jesus Christ. The question for all of us is what do we do with Jesus?

Let us read the rest of the Scripture quoted at the beginning of this chapter:

Beloved, believe not every spirit, but try the spirits whether they are of God: because many false prophets are gone out into the world.

Hereby know ye the Spirit of God: Every spirit that confesseth that Jesus Christ is come in the flesh is of God:

And every spirit that confesseth not that Jesus Christ is come in the flesh is not of God: and this is that spirit of antichrist, whereof ye have heard that it should come; and even now already is it in the world.

Ye are of God, little children, and have overcome them: because <u>greater is he that is in you, than he that is in the world</u>.

They are of the world: therefore speak they of the world, and the world heareth them.

We are of God: he that knoweth God heareth us; he that is not of God heareth not us. <u>Hereby know we the spirit of truth, and the spirit of error</u>. John 4:1-6

So, we now have a very accurate way to determine the Spirit of Truth and the spirit of error. The Holy Spirit is the Spirit of Truth and will <u>never</u> contradict the written Word of God. Dear reader, this point would be well worth remembering as you observe, read about, and hear of the many frenetic activities of the spirit of error in the world. You may very well have been caught up in a belief, activity, or "Religious" group that you have doubts about.

Let us continue the quote in order to learn more truth; truth that the world will not hear, but that those who are seeking after righteousness and the heart of God will.

Beloved, let us love one another: for love is of God; and every one that loveth is born of God, and knoweth God. He that loveth not knoweth not God; for God is love. In this was manifested the love of God toward us, because that <u>God sent his only begotten Son into the world, that we might live through him</u>.

Jesus is the way and only way of life. Why?

Herein is love, not that we loved God, but that <u>he loved us, and sent his Son to be the propitiation for our sins</u>.

He is the One and only One who died to pay the price of our sins.

37

Beloved, if God so loved us, <u>we ought also to love one another</u>. No man hath seen God at any time. <u>If we love one another, God dwelleth in us, and his love is perfected in us</u>.

The Spirit of Truth operates out of love. The spirit of error operates out of hatred. Those who oppress others and seek to coerce obedience to their religion are living by the sword and, unless they repent, will die by the sword. Those who live by violence toward others will be judged by God.

Hereby know we that we dwell in him, and he in us, because <u>he hath given us of his Spirit</u>.

His Spirit is the Holy Spirit, which is the Spirit of Truth!

And we have seen and do testify that <u>the Father sent the Son to be the Saviour of the world. Whosoever shall confess that Jesus is the Son of God, God dwelleth in him, and he in God</u>. 1 John 4:7-15

We now have a better understanding of difference between the Spirit of Truth and the spirit of error. The beloved apostle John, one of many eyewitnesses to the life, ministry, miracles, death, and resurrection of Jesus, records the following words of comfort and instruction spoken by our Lord and Savior:

Let not your heart be troubled: ye believe in God, <u>believe also in me</u>.

In my Father's house are many mansions: if it were not so, I would have told you. <u>I go to prepare a place for you</u>.

What an awesome future for every soul who repents and believes on the Lord Jesus!

And if I go and prepare a place for you, <u>I will come again, and receive you unto myself; that where I am, there ye may be also</u>.

What a wonderful promise to all who obey the truth!

And whither I go ye know, and <u>the way</u> ye know.

As we have learned already, <u>Jesus is the way</u>.

Thomas saith unto him, Lord, we know not whither thou goest; and how can we know the way?

Prior to the resurrection of Jesus, even His first disciples did not see or understand the truth.

Jesus saith unto him, <u>I am the way, the truth, and the life</u>: <u>no</u> man cometh unto the Father, but <u>by me</u>.

Not by Buddha, not by Confucius, not by Mohammed, not by religion, ritual, philanthropy, philosophy, knowledge, self-enlightenment, or any other man made doctrine.

If ye had <u>known me</u>, ye should have known my Father also: and from henceforth ye know him, and have seen him. Philip saith unto him, Lord, show us the Father, and it sufficeth us. Jesus saith unto him, Have I been so long time with you, and yet hast thou not known me, Philip? <u>he that hath seen me hath seen the Father</u>; and how sayest thou then, Show us the Father?

Jesus is the express image and exact representation of the character of God! *

Believest thou not that I am in the Father, and the Father in me? the words that I speak unto you I speak not of myself: but the Father that dwelleth in me, he doeth the works.

Just like the Holy Spirit in us, He "doith the works".

Believe me that I am in the Father, and the Father in me: or else believe me for the very works' sake. Verily, verily, I say unto you, He that believeth on me, the works that I do shall he do also; and greater works than these shall he do; because I go unto my Father. And whatsoever ye shall ask in my name, that will I do, that the Father may be glorified in the Son. If ye shall ask any thing in my name, I will do it. If ye love me, keep my commandments.

Here we have the full counsel of God and the Original Gospel, once delivered to the saints!

And I will pray the Father, and he shall give you another Comforter, that he may abide with you for ever;

What a wonderful blessing! The Holy Spirit is our Comforter and will remain in us and lead us into all truth. **

Even the Spirit of truth; whom the world cannot receive, because it seeth him not, neither knoweth him: but ye know him; for he dwelleth with you, and shall be in you.

The Holy Spirit in you is the Spirit of Truth!

I will not leave you comfortless: I will come to you. Yet a little while, and the world seeth me no more; but ye see me: because I live, ye shall live also.

This is the truth, even eternal life!

At that day ye shall know that I am in my Father, and ye in me, and I in you. He that hath my commandments, and keepeth them, he it is that loveth me: and he that loveth me shall be loved of my Father, and I will love him, and will manifest myself to him.

This is the True Gospel – if we obey, we are a testimony to the world that we are believers and truly love Jesus. He, in turn, will make Himself known to each of us.

Judas saith unto him, not Iscariot, Lord, how is it that thou wilt manifest thyself unto us, and not unto the world? Jesus answered and said unto him, If a man love me, he will keep my words: and my Father will love him, and we will come unto him, and make our abode with him.

Again, Jesus teaches us that, if we love Him, we will obey Him and He will reside in our hearts.

He that loveth me not keepeth not my sayings: and the word which ye hear is not mine, but the Father's which sent me.

This is such an important truth! We must understand that God the Father is the source of all wisdom and truth for all mankind. His way is the way of life.

These things have I spoken unto you, being yet present with you. But the Comforter, which is the Holy Ghost, whom the Father will send in my name, he shall teach you all things, and bring all things to your remembrance, whatsoever I have said unto you.

We do not need a priest or self-proclaimed spiritual leader to teach us the truth. We have the written Word of God in our hands and the author - the Holy Spirit - in our hearts. This should be a great comfort to all believers.

Peace I leave with you, my peace I give unto you: not as the world giveth, give I unto you. Let not your heart be troubled, neither let it be afraid.

Our Savior, the Son of God, is the Prince of Peace.

Ye have heard how I said unto you, I go away, and come again unto you. If ye loved me, ye would rejoice, because I said, I go unto the Father: for my Father is greater than I. And now I have told you before it come to pass, that, when it is come to pass, ye might believe. Hereafter I will not talk much with you: for the prince of this world cometh, and hath nothing in me.

This is Satan, the father of lies and of the children of disobedience.

But that the world may know that I love the Father; and as the Father gave me commandment, even so I do. Arise, let us go hence. John 14

In the preceding passage, I referred to the following two quotes so that we can learn two very important truths:

* God, who at sundry times and in divers manners spake in time past unto the fathers by the prophets, Hath in these last days spoken unto us by his Son, whom he hath appointed heir of all things, by whom also he made the worlds; Who being the brightness of his glory, and the express image of his person, and upholding all things by the word of his power, when he had by himself purged our sins, sat down on the right hand of the Majesty on high: Being made so much better than the

angels, as he hath by inheritance obtained a more excellent name than they. Hebrews 1:1-4

** I have yet many things to say unto you, but ye cannot bear them now. Howbeit when he, <u>the Spirit of truth</u>, is come, <u>he will guide you into all truth</u>: for <u>he shall not speak of himself</u>; but <u>whatsoever he shall hear, that shall he speak</u>: and he will shew you things to come. <u>He shall glorify me</u>: for he shall receive of mine, and shall shew it unto you. John 16:12-14

- Jesus is the exact image of the character of God. He is Emmanuel – God with us!
- The Holy Spirit is THE Spirit of Truth. He will be our guide and glorify Jesus!

There you have it, dear reader; the truth from the Spirit of Truth.

ANY person, organization, doctrine or philosophy that denigrates, diminishes, or outright denies the person of Jesus as the Son of God, who died for our sins, was resurrected, and now sits at the right hand of the Most High God, is manifesting the fruit of the spirit of error.

I would like to close this chapter with a quote from R.A. Torrey regarding the purpose of the Holy Spirit, which is the Spirit of Truth, in the life of every believer on the Lord Jesus:

"A true Christian life is a personally conducted life, conducted at every turn by a divine person. It is the believer's privilege to be absolutely set free from all care and worry and anxiety as to the decisions which he must make at any turn of his life. The Holy Spirit undertakes all that responsibility for us. A true Christian life is not one governed by a long set of rules without us, but led by a living and ever-present person within us. It is in this connection that Paul says, 'For ye received not the spirit of bondage again unto fear' (Rom. 8:15). R.A. Torry, *The Person and Work of the Holy Spirit.*

For as many as are <u>led by the Spirit of God</u>, <u>they are the sons of God</u>. For ye have not received the spirit of bondage again to fear; but ye have received <u>the Spirit of adoption</u>, whereby we cry, Abba, Father. Romans 8:14-15

This is what it means to be born again; born into the family of God.

Heavenly Father, I am wretched and You are Holy. Thank You, Father for sending Your beloved Son, Jesus to teach me the way and the truth, and thank You for providing a way for me to be forgiven for my sins and be adopted into Your family. Oh Jesus, I am so sorry that You had to suffer so terribly and sacrifice Your innocent life because of my sins. I repent of my way of living and confess my sins to You. Please wash me clean by Your shed blood and fill me with Your Holy Spirit. I want to walk in the truth. You died for me and I want to live for You. I love You Jesus and I invite you into my heart and life for all the days I am given on this earth. Amen.

Chapter 3

PETER THE FISHERMAN VERSUS PETER THE FISHER OF MEN

When Jesus came into the coasts of Caesarea Philippi, he asked his disciples, saying, Whom do men say that I the Son of man am? Matthew 16:13

Of all the questions that could be asked, knowing the correct answer to the one above is of utmost importance for all of us. Understanding exactly who Jesus is, and what that means, cannot be over emphasized for every living soul. Jesus had been with His disciples for a long time when He asked them. They responded:

Some say that thou art John the Baptist: some, Elias; and others, Jeremias, or one of the prophets. Matthew 16:14

Jesus then asked them directly:

He saith unto them, But <u>whom say ye that I am</u>? Matthew 16:15

This is THE question of all questions. It is the one that has been asked an untold number of times by an uncountable number of souls. Answering it correctly has, and always will be, the highest priority for anyone searching for the truth. It was a very direct question and, amazingly, after all that His closest followers had heard Jesus teach and all the miracles they had seen Him do, eleven of them got the answer wrong. Please understand, I am not blaming or judging them. If we put ourselves in their shoes, we would have come to the same conclusion. Many still get it wrong today for the same reason they did. The motivations and attitudes of the heart of those answering the question were then, and still are, in the wrong place.

The only reason that one of the twelve answered correctly was that the answer was revealed to him by God, the Father.

And Simon Peter answered and said, Thou art the Christ, the Son of the living God. And Jesus answered and said unto him, Blessed art thou, Simon Barjona: for flesh and blood <u>hath not</u> revealed it unto thee, but <u>my Father which is in heaven</u>. Matthew 16:16-17

So, it is here we learn that God Himself gave Peter the truth about who Jesus was. Let us investigate the story of this disciple and discover the magnitude of the effect that knowing Jesus had on his life.

Do you know what Peter's response was after encountering Jesus for the first time? Many do not. Certainly, the promoters of Catholicism would prefer that you remain ignorant, as they teach the man-made doctrine of the papacy and that Peter was the first so called "Pope". When Peter met Jesus, this is what happened:

And it came to pass, that, as the people pressed upon him (Jesus) to hear the word of God, he stood by the lake of Gennesaret, And saw two ships standing by the lake: but the fishermen were gone out of them, and were washing their nets. And he entered into one of the ships, which was Simon's, and prayed him that he would thrust out a little from the land. And

46

he sat down, and taught the people out of the ship. **Now when he had left speaking, he said unto Simon, Launch out into the deep, and let down your nets for a draught. And Simon answering said unto him, Master, we have toiled all the night, and have taken nothing: nevertheless at thy word I will let down the net. And when they had this done, they inclosed a great multitude of fishes: and their net brake. And they beckoned unto their partners, which were in the other ship, that they should come and help them. And they came, and filled both the ships, so that they began to sink. <u>When Simon Peter saw it, he fell down at Jesus' knees, saying, Depart from me; for I am a sinful man, O Lord</u>. For he was astonished, and all that were with him, at the draught of the fishes which they had taken: And so was also James, and John, the sons of Zebedee, which were partners with Simon. <u>And Jesus said unto Simon, Fear not; from henceforth thou shalt catch men</u>. And when they had brought their ships to land, <u>they forsook all, and followed him</u>.** Luke 5:1-11

Peter, having just heard Jesus teaching the people, now sees His miraculous power and realizes he is in the presence of a Holy man. So, what does he do? He falls down at the feet of the Jesus and confesses that he is a sinner! This is the same response all who are seeking the truth have when they meet Jesus. After returning to shore, Peter and his fishing partners leave their boats, nets, and everything else to follow Him. It would not be an overstatement to say that Peter's life was radically changed after meeting Jesus!

Returning to the revelation of the truth spoken by Peter regarding the identity of Jesus, the propagators of Catholicism, who claim that Peter was the first of their self-proclaimed "Infallible Popes," also do not want you to know what happened right after God honored Peter with the truth about Jesus. Dear reader, we must remember that the Scriptures have been given by God through men inspired by the Holy Spirit and will always be properly interpreted within the context of what is written. In other words, the Scriptures bear witness to the Scriptures and are not subject to any private interpretation.

All scripture is given <u>by inspiration of God</u>, and is profitable <u>for doctrine</u>, <u>for reproof</u>, <u>for correction</u>, <u>for instruction in righteousness</u>: That the man of God may be perfect, thoroughly furnished unto all good works. 2 Timothy 3:16-17

So, no sooner had Peter been blessed to know the truth regarding Jesus, than he was soundly rebuked by the Lord for trying to prevent Him from going to Jerusalem!

From that time forth began Jesus to shew unto his disciples, how that he must go unto Jerusalem, and suffer many things of the elders and chief priests and scribes, <u>and be killed</u>, <u>and be raised again the third day</u>. Then Peter took him, and began to rebuke him, saying, Be it far from thee, Lord: this shall not be unto thee. But he turned, and said unto Peter, <u>Get thee behind me, Satan: thou art an offence unto me</u>: for thou savourest not the things that be of God, <u>but those that be of men</u>. Then said Jesus unto his disciples, <u>If any man will come after me, let him deny himself, and take up his cross, and follow me</u>. Matthew 16:21-24

If Jesus had not gone to Jerusalem, He would not have been crucified for our sins and we would all be lost. The cross was the ultimate mission of Jesus in the world. It was by and through the cross that God reconciled man to Himself.

Now we know that what things soever the law saith, it saith to them who are under the law: that <u>every mouth may be stopped, and all the world may become guilty before God</u>.

There will be no excuses at the judgment. We are all guilty.

Therefore by the deeds of the law there <u>shall no flesh be justified in his sight</u>: for <u>by the law is the knowledge of sin</u>. But now <u>the righteousness of God without the law</u> is manifested, being witnessed by the law and the prophets; Even the righteousness of God which is <u>by faith of Jesus Christ unto all and upon all them that believe</u>: for there is no difference: <u>For all have sinned, and come short of the glory of God</u>; <u>Being justified freely by his grace through the redemption that is in Christ Jesus</u>: Whom God hath set forth to be a propitiation (an offering to satisfy the holiness of God by paying the penalty of our sin) **<u>through faith in his blood</u>, to declare his righteousness for the remission of sins <u>that are past</u>, through the forbearance of God; To declare, I say, at this time his righteousness: that he might be just, and <u>the justifier of him which believeth in Jesus</u>. Romans 3:19-26**

So, in reality, at that moment Peter was acting as an agent of Satan. Who is it that opposes all that God stands for and who is it that opposes God's plans for the salvation of mankind? Satan. He is the fallen angel Lucifer. Peter demonstrates here that <u>it is very easy to be deceived if we rely on our own wisdom instead of God's</u>. Do not be deceived. There is only One who can save. There is only One who offered Himself up as the perfect sacrifice for all by laying down His sinless life so that we might have forgiveness and be reconciled to a Holy God. There is only One who is God, became a man, died for our sins, was buried, resurrected, and lives now and forever as our Lord and Savior to all who come to Him. His name is Jesus.

Returning to our story with Peter, we are now in the Garden of Gethsemane, just outside Jerusalem, and the Jewish religious leaders have come to arrest Jesus; when they do, all of His followers (those who had been with Him for three years - including Peter) run away in fear. Jesus had already prophesied that they would all abandon Him and specifically singled out Peter as the one who would deny three times even knowing Him. He spoke this prophecy right after Peter had just said he would stand by Him!

And Jesus saith unto them, All ye shall be offended because of me this night: for it is written, I will smite the shepherd, and the sheep shall be scattered. But after that I am risen, I will go before you into Galilee. But Peter said unto him, Although all shall be offended, yet will not I. And Jesus saith unto him, Verily I say unto thee, That this day, even in this night, before the cock crow twice, thou shalt deny me thrice. Mark 14:27-32

Rise up, let us go; lo, he that betrayeth me is at hand. And immediately, while he yet spake, cometh Judas, one of the twelve, and with him a great multitude with swords and staves, from the chief priests and the scribes and the elders. And he that betrayed him had given them a token, saying, Whomsoever I shall kiss, that same is he; take him, and lead him away safely. And as soon as he was come, he goeth straightway to him, and saith, Master, master; and kissed him. And they laid their hands on him, and took him. And one of them that stood by drew a sword, and smote a servant of the high priest, and cut off his ear. And Jesus answered and said unto them, Are ye come out, as against a thief, with swords and with staves to take me? I was daily with you in the temple teaching, and ye took me not: but the scriptures must be fulfilled. And they all forsook him, and fled. Mark 14:42-50

These words of Jesus, like all His words, came to pass with total accuracy. This was a dark moment for all of His disciples, as they faced the reality of their betrayal of the Lord; despite their assurances to Him that they would not abandon Him. All their hopes seemed to have been dashed in a heartbeat. The One whom they had so closely followed for three years and the One who's astounding teaching and miracles they had been eye witnesses to, was now being led away to be tried and executed. An innocent man in whom they had left everything to follow, and in whom they had placed all of their hope, was now being led away to die. Had they been listening to and believing what Jesus had already told them, they would not have been surprised at this turn of events.

We now proceed to Jerusalem where Peter is standing outside the palace of the high priest as Jesus is being put on trial by the Jewish leaders. After witnessing the shocking arrest of their Master and having now abandoned Him to their great shame, the final blow for Peter is about to occur.

And as Peter was beneath in the palace, there cometh one of the maids of the high priest: And when she saw Peter warming himself, she looked upon him, and said, And thou also wast with Jesus of Nazareth. But <u>he denied, saying, I know not, neither understand I what thou sayest</u>. And he went out into the porch; and the cock crew. And a maid saw him again, and began to say to them that stood by, This is one of them. And <u>he denied it again</u>. And a little after, they that stood by said again to Peter, Surely thou art one of them: for thou art a Galilaean, and thy speech agreeth thereto. But <u>he began to curse and to swear, saying, I know not this man of whom ye speak</u>. And the second time the cock crew. And Peter called to mind the word that Jesus said unto him, Before the cock crow twice, thou shalt deny me thrice. <u>And when he thought thereon, he wept</u>. Mark 14:66-72

Dear reader, the disciple Peter is very close to my own heart and maybe yours as well. I understand the passion in Peter's spirit.

Like him, I also want to be where the truth is and where the love is. To my own shame, there have been many times in my life where I have "Shot first and asked questions later!" I too have experienced colossal failures, false starts, and sins which I mournfully regret. There were many times when I really made a mess of things. I sincerely empathize with the pain in Peter's heart at this moment, and how much it must have hurt him to know he betrayed his Lord.

Thanks be to our God, though, for His abundant tender mercies and loving kindnesses granted to all who turn to Him with a contrite and humble heart.

For thus saith the high and lofty One that inhabiteth eternity, whose name is Holy; I dwell in the high and holy place, with him also that is of a contrite and humble spirit, to revive the spirit of the humble, and to revive the heart of the contrite ones. Isaiah 57:15

We now move forward to the third day after Jesus was crucified and, having found His tomb empty, Peter and the other disciples return home in confusion. They still did not understand the teachings of Jesus that He must suffer and die for the sins of mankind, and on the third day He would rise again.

The first day of the week cometh Mary Magdalene early, when it was yet dark, unto the sepulchre, and seeth the stone taken away from the sepulchre. Then she runneth, and cometh to Simon Peter, and to the other disciple, whom Jesus loved, and saith unto them, They have taken away the LORD out of the sepulchre, and we know not where they have laid him. Peter therefore went forth, and that other disciple, and came to the sepulchre. So they ran both together: and the other disciple did outrun Peter, and came first to the sepulchre. And he stooping down, and looking in, saw the linen clothes lying; yet went he

not in. **Then cometh Simon Peter following him, and went into the sepulchre, and seeth the linen clothes lie, And the napkin, that was about his head, not lying with the linen clothes, but wrapped together in a place by itself. Then went in also that other disciple, which came first to the sepulchre, and he saw, and believed.** <u>**For as yet they knew not the scripture, that he must rise again from the dead**</u>**. Then the disciples went away again unto their own home. John 20:1-10**

A short time later, after Jesus had shown Himself alive again to His followers, Peter and some of the disciples decide to go fishing. Here we pick up the story:

After these things Jesus shewed himself again to the disciples at the sea of Tiberias; and on this wise shewed he himself. There were together Simon Peter, and Thomas called Didymus, and Nathanael of Cana in Galilee, and the sons of Zebedee, and two other of his disciples. Simon Peter saith unto them, I go a fishing. They say unto him, We also go with thee. They went forth, and entered into a ship immediately; and that night they caught nothing. But when the morning was now come, Jesus stood on the shore: but the disciples knew not that it was Jesus. Then Jesus saith unto them, Children, have ye any meat? They answered him, No. And he said unto them, Cast the net on the right side of the ship, and ye shall find. They cast therefore, and now they were not able to draw it for the multitude of fishes. Therefore that disciple whom Jesus loved saith unto Peter, It is the Lord. Now when Simon Peter heard that it was the Lord, he girt his fisher's coat unto him, (for he was naked,) and did cast himself into the sea. And the other disciples came in a little ship; (for they were not far from land, but as it were two hundred cubits,) dragging the net with fishes. As soon then as they were come to land, they saw a fire of coals there, and fish laid thereon, and bread. Jesus saith unto them, Bring of

the fish which ye have now caught. Simon Peter went up, and drew the net to land full of great fishes, an hundred and fifty and three: and for all there were so many, yet was not the net broken. Jesus saith unto them, Come and dine. And none of the disciples durst ask him, Who art thou? knowing that it was the Lord. Jesus then cometh, and taketh bread, and giveth them, and fish likewise. <u>This is now the third time that Jesus shewed himself to his disciples, after that he was risen from the dead.</u> So when they had dined, Jesus saith to Simon Peter, <u>Simon, son of Jonas, lovest thou me more than these</u>? He saith unto him, Yea, Lord; thou knowest that I love thee. He saith unto him, Feed my lambs. He saith to him again the second time, <u>Simon, son of Jonas, lovest thou me</u>? He saith unto him, Yea, Lord; thou knowest that I love thee. He saith unto him, Feed my sheep. He saith unto him the third time, <u>Simon, son of Jonas, lovest thou me</u>? Peter was grieved because he said unto him the third time, Lovest thou me? And he said unto him, Lord, thou knowest all things; thou knowest that I love thee. Jesus saith unto him, Feed my sheep. Verily, verily, I say unto thee, When thou wast young, thou girdest thyself, and walkedst whither thou wouldest: <u>but when thou shalt be old, thou shalt stretch forth thy hands, and another shall gird thee, and carry thee whither thou wouldest not. This spake he, signifying by what death he should glorify God.</u> And when he had spoken this, he saith unto him, <u>Follow me.</u> John 21:1-19

Here we see the amazing grace and mercy of our God! Jesus, the risen Savior, publically restores Peter to the office of apostle and, in addition, makes a prophetic statement regarding the death of Peter and how that death would honor God. From this point on, as we shall see, Peter the fisherman serves his Master as Peter the fisher of men!

After appearing in the flesh to many of His followers and prior to ascending back to Heaven, Jesus tells them to remain in Jerusalem until they receive the baptism of the Holy Spirit, which He had previously promised them. The beloved physician, Luke writes in Acts:

The former treatise (the Gospel of Luke) **have I made, O Theophilus, of all that Jesus began both to do and teach, Until the day in which he was taken up, after that he through the Holy Ghost had given commandments unto the apostles whom he had chosen: To whom also he shewed himself alive after his passion by many infallible proofs, being seen of them forty days, and speaking of the things pertaining to the kingdom of God: And, being assembled together with them, commanded them that they should not depart from Jerusalem, but wait for the promise of the Father, which, saith he, ye have heard of me. For John truly baptized with water; but <u>ye shall be baptized with the Holy Ghost not many days hence</u>. Acts 1:1-5**

Now we see the awesome power of God, through His Holy Spirit, work in the life of Peter with the result that the fisherman's nets become full to overflowing!

And when the day of Pentecost was fully come, they were all with one accord in one place. And suddenly there came a sound from heaven as of a rushing mighty wind, and it filled all the house where they were sitting. And there appeared unto them cloven tongues like as of fire, and it sat upon each of them.

And <u>they were all filled with the Holy Ghost</u>, and began to speak with other tongues, as the Spirit gave them utterance. And there were dwelling at Jerusalem Jews, devout men, out of every nation under heaven. Now when this was noised abroad,

the multitude came together, and were confounded, because that every man heard them speak in his own language. And they were all amazed and marvelled, saying one to another, Behold, are not all these which speak Galilaeans? And <u>how hear we every man in our own tongue, wherein we were born</u>?

This is what the Spirit of Truth manifests in those with the gift of speaking in tongues. It is a sign for unbelievers who will understand the words being spoken (<u>warning</u> - this gift has been abused and counterfeited by those operating under the influence of the spirit of error).

Parthians, and Medes, and Elamites, and the dwellers in Mesopotamia, and in Judaea, and Cappadocia, in Pontus, and Asia, Phrygia, and Pamphylia, in Egypt, and in the parts of Libya about Cyrene, and strangers of Rome, Jews and proselytes, Cretes and Arabians, <u>we do hear them speak in our tongues the wonderful works of God</u>. And they were all amazed, and were in doubt, saying one to another, What meaneth this? Others mocking said, These men are full of new wine.

Now we listen to the words of Peter, the fisher of men:

But <u>Peter</u>, standing up with the eleven, lifted up his voice, and said unto them, Ye men of Judaea, and all ye that dwell at Jerusalem, be this known unto you, and hearken to my words: For these are not drunken, as ye suppose, seeing it is but the third hour of the day. But this is that which was spoken by the prophet Joel; And it shall come to pass in the last days, saith God, <u>I will pour out of my Spirit upon all flesh</u>: and your sons and your daughters shall prophesy, and your young men shall see visions, and your old men shall dream dreams: And on my servants and on my handmaidens <u>I will pour out in those days</u>

56

of my Spirit; and they shall prophesy: And I will shew wonders in heaven above, and signs in the earth beneath; blood, and fire, and vapour of smoke: The sun shall be turned into darkness, and the moon into blood, before the great and notable day of the Lord come: And it shall come to pass, that whosoever shall call on the name of the Lord shall be saved. Ye men of Israel, hear these words; Jesus of Nazareth, a man approved of God among you by miracles and wonders and signs, which God did by him in the midst of you, as ye yourselves also know: Him, being delivered by the determinate counsel and foreknowledge of God, ye have taken, and by wicked hands have crucified and slain: Whom God hath raised up, having loosed the pains of death: because it was not possible that he should be holden of it. For David speaketh concerning him, I foresaw the Lord always before my face, for he is on my right hand, that I should not be moved: Therefore did my heart rejoice, and my tongue was glad; moreover also my flesh shall rest in hope: Because thou wilt not leave my soul in hell, neither wilt thou suffer thine Holy One to see corruption. Thou hast made known to me the ways of life; thou shalt make me full of joy with thy countenance. Men and brethren, let me freely speak unto you of the patriarch David, that he is both dead and buried, and his sepulchre is with us unto this day. Therefore being a prophet, and knowing that God had sworn with an oath to him, that of the fruit of his loins, according to the flesh, he would raise up Christ to sit on his throne; He seeing this before spake of the resurrection of Christ, that his soul was not left in hell, neither his flesh did see corruption. This Jesus hath God raised up, whereof we all are witnesses. Therefore being by the right hand of God exalted, and having received of the Father the promise of the Holy Ghost, he hath shed forth this, which ye now see and hear. For David is not ascended into the heavens: but he saith himself, The Lord said unto my Lord, Sit thou on my right hand, Until

I make thy foes thy footstool. **Therefore let all the house of Israel know assuredly, that <u>God hath made the same Jesus, whom ye have crucified, both Lord and Christ</u>. Now when they heard this, <u>they were pricked in their heart, and said unto Peter and to the rest of the apostles, Men and brethren, what shall we do</u>? Then <u>Peter</u> said unto them, <u>Repent</u>, and <u>be baptized every one of you in the name of Jesus Christ for the remission of sins</u>, and <u>ye shall receive the gift of the Holy Ghost</u>. For the <u>promise</u> is unto you, and to your children, and to all that are afar off, even as many as the LORD our God shall call. And <u>with many other words did he testify and exhort</u>, saying, Save yourselves from this untoward generation. Then they that gladly received his word were baptized: and <u>the same day there were added unto them about three thousand souls</u>.** Acts 2:1-41

Wow! Peter the impulsive, Peter the coward, Peter the denier of Jesus, has just preached the truth by the power of the Holy Spirit in him and three thousand were converted! What we are learning here should build the faith of all who believe in Jesus and have made Him their Lord and Savior!

As we continue, take note of the power of the Holy Spirit in Peter, and how with great boldness accompanied by irrefutable miracles, he testifies to the true Gospel of Jesus Christ, even at great personal risk.

Now Peter and John went up together into the temple at the hour of prayer, being the ninth hour. And a certain man lame from his mother's womb was carried, whom they laid daily at the gate of the temple which is called Beautiful, to ask alms of them that entered into the temple; Who seeing Peter and John about to go into the temple asked an alms. And Peter, fastening his eyes upon him with John, said, Look on us. And he gave

heed unto them, expecting to receive something of them. <u>Then Peter said</u>, Silver and gold have I none; but such as I have give I thee: <u>In the name of Jesus Christ of Nazareth rise up and walk</u>. And he took him by the right hand, and lifted him up: and immediately his feet and ankle bones received strength. And he leaping up stood, and walked, and entered with them into the temple, walking, and leaping, and praising God. And all the people saw him walking and praising God: And they knew that it was he which sat for alms at the Beautiful gate of the temple: and they were filled with wonder and amazement at that which had happened unto him. And as the lame man which was healed held Peter and John, all the people ran together unto them in the porch that is called Solomon's, greatly wondering. And when <u>Peter</u> saw it, <u>he answered unto the people</u>, Ye men of Israel, why marvel ye at this? or why look ye so earnestly on us, as though by our own power or holiness we had made this man to walk? The God of Abraham, and of Isaac, and of Jacob, the God of our father<u>s, hath glorified his Son Jesus; whom ye delivered up</u>, and denied him in the presence of Pilate, when he was determined to let him go. <u>But ye denied the Holy One and the Just</u>, and desired a murderer to be granted unto you; <u>And killed the Prince of life</u>, whom God hath raised from the dead; whereof we are witnesses. And his name through faith in his name hath made this man strong, whom ye see and know: yea, the faith which is by him hath given him this perfect soundness in the presence of you all. And now, brethren, <u>I wot</u> (know) <u>that through ignorance ye did it, as did also your rulers</u>. But those things, which God before had shewed by the mouth of all his prophets, that Christ should suffer, he hath so fulfilled. <u>Repent</u> ye therefore, and <u>be converted</u>, that <u>your sins may be blotted out</u>, when the times of refreshing shall come from the presence of the Lord. Acts 3:1-19

This, beloved saints, is the boldness of the Spirit of Truth speaking through the fisher of men!

Continuing the story of Peter and John's confrontation with the religious leaders of Israel, the latter took hold of the two apostles as we see in the following Scriptures:

And as they spake unto the people, the priests, and the captain of the temple, and the Sadducees, came upon them, Being grieved that they taught the people, and preached through Jesus the resurrection from the dead. And they laid hands on them, and put them in hold unto the next day: for it was now eventide. Howbeit <u>many of them which heard the word believed</u>; and the number of the men was about <u>five thousand</u>.

Five thousand more believers!

And it came to pass on the morrow, that their <u>rulers</u>, and <u>elders</u>, and <u>scribes</u>, And <u>Annas the high priest</u>, and <u>Caiaphas</u>, and <u>John</u>, and <u>Alexander</u>, and <u>as many as were of the kindred of the high priest</u>, were gathered together at Jerusalem. And when they had set them in the midst, they asked, By what power, or by what name, have ye done this?

What sort of man is Peter now? Is he a denier of the Savior? No, he is a bold contender for the faith!

Please read the words he spoke next very carefully.

Then <u>Peter, filled with the Holy Ghost</u>, said unto them, Ye rulers of the people, and elders of Israel, If we this day be examined of the good deed done to the impotent man, by what means he is made whole; <u>Be it known unto you all, and to all the people of Israel, that by the name of Jesus Christ of</u>

Nazareth, whom ye crucified, whom God raised from the dead, even by him doth this man stand here before you whole. This is the stone which was set at nought of you builders, which is become the head of the corner. Neither is there salvation in any other: for there is none other name under heaven given among men, whereby we must be saved. Now when they saw the boldness of Peter and John, and perceived that they were unlearned and ignorant men, they marvelled; and they took knowledge of them, that they had been with Jesus. And beholding the man which was healed standing with them, they could say nothing against it. But when they had commanded them to go aside out of the council, they conferred among themselves, Saying, What shall we do to these men? for that indeed a notable miracle hath been done by them is manifest to all them that dwell in Jerusalem; and we cannot deny it. But that it spread no further among the people, let us straitly threaten them, that they speak henceforth to no man in this name. And they called them, and commanded them not to speak at all nor teach in the name of Jesus.

How do Peter and John respond? Like men of God!

But Peter and John answered and said unto them, Whether it be right in the sight of God to hearken unto you more than unto God, judge ye. For we cannot but speak the things which we have seen and heard. So when they had further threatened them, they let them go, finding nothing how they might punish them, because of the people: for all men glorified God for that which was done. For the man was above forty years old, on whom this miracle of healing was shewed. And being let go, they went to their own company, and reported all that the chief priests and elders had said unto them. Acts 4:1-23

We now see the extraordinary effect meeting Jesus has had in the man Peter! This man was radically changed and he lived the rest of his life serving his first love, Savior, and Lord! Historical records document that Peter was martyred in Rome for his faith in Jesus. Peter fulfills the testimony of Jesus many years earlier regarding the apostle's death by laying down his life for his Lord:

"Among many other saints, the blessed apostle Peter was condemned to death, and crucified, as some do write, at Rome; albeit some others, and not without cause, do doubt thereof. Hegesippus saith that Nero sought matter against Peter to put him to death; which, when the people perceived, they entreated Peter with much ado that he would fly the city. Peter, through their importunity at length persuaded, prepared himself to avoid. But, coming to the gate, he saw the Lord Christ come to meet him, to whom he, worshipping, said, "Lord, whither dost Thou go?" To whom He answered and said, "I am come again to be crucified." By this, Peter, perceiving his suffering to be understood, returned into the city. Jerome saith that he was crucified, his head being down and his feet upward, himself so requiring, because he was (he said) unworthy to be crucified after the same form and manner as the Lord was." - John Foxe, *Foxe's Book of Martyrs*

Dear reader, this brutal death of Peter, was his greatest victory! He sealed his testimony with his own blood and left it for all future generations; you, me and anyone who is seeking the truth.

What did Jesus say?

For there is nothing covered, that shall not be revealed; neither hid, that shall not be known. Therefore whatsoever ye have spoken in darkness <u>shall be heard in the light</u>; and that which ye have spoken in the ear in closets <u>shall be proclaimed upon the housetops</u>. And I say unto you <u>my friends</u>, <u>Be not afraid of</u>

them that kill the body, and after that have no more that they can do. But I will forewarn you whom ye shall fear: Fear him, which after he hath killed hath power to cast into hell; yea, I say unto you, Fear him. Are not five sparrows sold for two farthings, and not one of them is forgotten before God? But even the very hairs of your head are all numbered. Fear not therefore: **ye are of more value than many sparrows.** Also I say unto you, **Whosoever shall confess me before men, him shall the Son of man also confess before the angels of God: But he that denieth me before men shall be denied before the angels of God.** Luke 12:2-9

There will be no allowance for hypocrisy at the judgment. Every mouth will be closed. Peter lived by faith, and he died by the same faith in the only One who can save. He denied himself, picked up his cross, and followed Jesus to the end of his earthly life. He is now with his Lord in glory and has inherited eternal life! Peter was a true "Overcomer!"

Knowing the story of Peter should be a powerful inspiration to all of us who believe and it should build our faith in the truth of Jesus. He is the solid rock on which to stand. If you have never met Jesus, consider the actions of Peter's life. No man would choose to die for a lie, but the greatest gift a man can give is to lay his life down for a friend. Peter followed the life and teaching of his Master. As Jesus lived, so He taught His followers to do the same.

Jesus said:

This is my commandment, That ye love one another, as I have loved you. Greater love hath no man than this, that a man lay down his life for his friends. Ye are my friends, if ye do whatsoever I command you. John 15:12-14

I would like to end this chapter honoring the other apostles and eyewitnesses of Jesus who also laid down their lives and proved their faith by their actions. Just as Peter did, they made the decision to obey the truth by their deeds and are now with the Lord Jesus; never to be apart from Him again. These men gave everything for Jesus. I do not know about you, but when I read about saints like these, it shames me as I consider the times in the past when I lived for myself. It also strengthens my spirit and faith to see such men of courage lay down their lives for the truth. These heroes of the faith left a legacy of love that should inspire all of us to good works.

Again, we turn to *Foxe's Book of Martyrs* for the historical accounts:

Stephen

His death was occasioned by the faithful manner in which he preached the Gospel to the betrayers and murderers of Christ. To such a degree of madness were they excited, that they cast him out of the city and stoned him to death. The time when he suffered is generally supposed to have been at the Passover which succeeded to that of our Lord's crucifixion, and to the era of his ascension, in the following spring. Upon this a great persecution was raised against all who professed their belief in Christ as the Messiah, or as a prophet. We are immediately told by St. Luke, that "there was a great persecution against the church which was at Jerusalem;" and that "they were all scattered abroad throughout the regions of Judaea and Samaria, except the apostles." About two thousand Christians, with Nicanor, one of the seven deacons, suffered martyrdom during the "persecution that arose about Stephen.

Andrew

The brother of Peter. He preached the gospel to many Asiatic nations; but on his arrival at Edessa he was taken and crucified on a cross, the two ends of which were fixed transversely in the ground. Hence the derivation of the term, St. Andrew's Cross.

Mark

Born of Jewish parents of the tribe of Levi. He is supposed to have been converted to Christianity by Peter, whom he served as an amanuensis (one who is employed to copy manuscript), and under whose inspection he wrote his Gospel in the Greek language. Mark was dragged to pieces by the people of Alexandria, at the great solemnity of Serapis their idol, ending his life under their merciless hands.

Jude

The brother of James, was commonly called Thaddeus. He was crucified at Edessa, A.D. 72.

Bartholomew

Preached in several countries, and having translated the Gospel of Matthew into the language of India, he propagated it in that country. He was at length cruelly beaten and then crucified by the impatient idolaters.

Thomas

Called Didymus, preached the Gospel in Parthia and India, where exciting the rage of the pagan priests, he was martyred by being thrust through with a spear.

Luke

The evangelist, was the author of the Gospel which goes under his name. He travelled with Paul through various countries, and is supposed to have been hanged on an olive tree, by the idolatrous priests of Greece.

Simon

Surnamed Zelotes, preached the Gospel in Mauritania, Africa, and even in Britain, in which latter country he was crucified, A.D. 74.

John

The "beloved disciple," was brother to James the Great. The churches of Smyrna, Pergamos, Sardis, Philadelphia, Laodicea, and Thyatira, were founded by him. From Ephesus he was ordered to be sent to Rome, where it is affirmed he was cast into a cauldron of boiling oil. He escaped by miracle, without injury. Domitian afterwards banished him to the Isle of Patmos, where he wrote the Book of Revelation. Nerva, the successor of Domitian, recalled him. He was the only apostle who escaped a violent death.

Barnabas

Was of Cyprus, but of Jewish descent, his death is supposed to have taken place about A.D. 73.

And yet, notwithstanding all these continual persecutions and horrible punishments, the Church daily increased, deeply rooted in the doctrine of the apostles and of men apostolical, and watered plenteously with the blood of saints. – John Foxe, *Foxe's Book of Martyrs*

Dear reader, I am humbled when I consider the men and women who gave their own lives because of their faith in and love for Jesus. I am shamed when I consider the times that I complained and grumbled about all the light afflictions I have had to endure. They are nothing compared to what these dear saints accomplished. The following Scriptures speak to my heart:

Wherefore seeing we also are compassed about with so great a cloud of witnesses, let us lay aside every weight, and the sin which doth so easily beset us, and <u>let us run with patience</u> the race that is set before us, <u>Looking unto Jesus the author and finisher of our faith;</u>...<u>Ye have not yet resisted unto blood, striving against sin</u>. And ye have forgotten the exhortation which speaketh unto you as unto children, My son, despise not thou the chastening of the Lord, nor faint when thou art rebuked of him: <u>For whom the Lord loveth he chasteneth, and scourgeth every son whom he receiveth</u>. Hebrews 12:1-6

Heavenly Father, I fall down before You in all humility. I am shamed by the fact that so many of Your faithful servants shed their own blood as a testimony to the living faith that they had in Your precious Son, Jesus. Oh Father, please forgive me for any and all complaining and grumbling on my part, and for the times I walked selfishly in the past. Father, wash me clean again and create in me a new heart. Fill me afresh with Your Holy Spirit and sanctify me that I may bear much good fruit; to Your glory and that of the King of Kings, Jesus. Amen.

Chapter 4

BONDAGE VERSUS REBELLION

Stand fast therefore in the liberty wherewith Christ hath made us free, and be not entangled again with the yoke of bondage. Galatians 5:1

Dear reader, the Holy Bible is God's love letter to all of us. It tells us who God is, who we are, and what His intended plans are for us. From the Scriptures, we learn that God is Holy and we, through transgression, are not. Because God is Holy, He is also just. That means that we, who He created in His image and likeness, will be accountable to him for how we live our lives. When our lives on this earth are over, we will stand at the judgment and give an account of the time we spent here.

And as it is appointed unto men <u>once to die</u>, but after this the judgment: Hebrews 9:27

The bad news is, we have all sinned and as a result, have brought the sentence of death on our souls. The good news is that God loves us so much that He made provisions for the payment for the penalty of our sins. That payment is the shed blood of His innocent Son, Jesus. Through the Son's obedience, we all have the way of reconciliation to the Father open for us.

Therefore as by the offence of one (Adam) **judgment came upon all men to condemnation; even so by the righteousness of**

one (Jesus) **the free gift came upon all men unto justification of life. For as by one man's** <u>disobedience</u> **many were made sinners, so by the** <u>obedience</u> **of one shall many be made righteous. Romans 5:18-19**

After being baptized by John the Baptist, Jesus went into the wilderness for forty days. There He <u>fasted,</u> <u>prayed</u> and <u>overcame</u> the temptations of Satan. When He returned to His hometown of Nazareth, He went into the Synagogue and spoke these amazing words which absolutely astonished those listening:

And Jesus returned in the power of the Spirit into Galilee: and there went out a fame of him through all the region round about. And he taught in their synagogues, being glorified of all. And he came to Nazareth, where he had been brought up: and, as his custom was, he went into the synagogue on the sabbath day, and stood up for to read. And there was delivered unto him the book of the prophet Esaias. And when he had opened the book, he found the place where it was written,

The <u>**Spirit of the Lord**</u> (the Spirit of Truth) **is upon me, because he hath anointed me to** <u>**preach the gospel**</u> (the good news**) to the poor**; **he hath sent me to** <u>**heal the brokenhearted**</u>, **to** <u>**preach deliverance to the captives**</u>, **and** <u>**recovering of sight to the blind**</u>, **to** <u>**set at liberty them that are bruised**</u>, **To** <u>**preach the acceptable year of the Lord**</u>. **And he closed the book, and he gave it again to the minister, and sat down. And the eyes of all them that were in the synagogue were fastened on him. And he began to say unto them,** <u>**This day is this scripture fulfilled in your ears**</u>. **Luke 4:14-21**

What are we to learn from these words? Jesus is proclaiming the good news to mankind. He has come to free us from our captivity.

You may be asking yourself the same question that those who heard the words of Jesus asked Him:

Then said Jesus to those Jews which believed on him, <u>If ye continue in my word</u>, then are ye my disciples indeed; And ye shall know the truth, and <u>the truth shall make you free</u>. They answered him, We be Abraham's seed, and were never in bondage to any man: how sayest thou, Ye shall be made free? Jesus answered them, Verily, verily, I say unto you, <u>Whosoever committeth sin is the servant of sin</u>. John 8:31-34

Please read that last statement again and let it sink into your heart!

Whoever commits sin is the servant of sin!

Now we know what Jesus meant when He proclaimed that He would set free those who are captive, bruised and under the yoke of bondage. Jesus is speaking about <u>captivity to sin</u>. It is extremely critical that you understand, dear reader, the liberty we have in Jesus IS NOT A LICENSE TO SIN! In other words, Jesus did not set us free <u>to sin</u>, but free <u>from sin</u>. I must restate this truth again, and do so clearly, as there is <u>much</u> false teaching today regarding this central doctrine of the Christian faith!

Tragically, there are many who, with ever-itching ears, have welcomed the watered down, cheap grace, easy believing, no cost version of Christian faith promoted by wolves in sheep's clothing; a version built upon the idea that once a person makes a decision to "Accept Christ", all his or her past <u>and future</u> sins have been forgiven and they are no longer responsible for any change in the way they live their lives.

Let us read more of the Scriptures, which come after the quote at the start of this chapter, and see whether or not the Word of God lines up with the idea that we can say we are Christians and then do as we please.

For, brethren, ye have been called unto liberty; only use not liberty for an occasion to the flesh, but by love serve one another. For all the law is fulfilled in one word, even in this; Thou shalt love thy neighbour as thyself. But if ye bite and devour one another, take heed that ye be not consumed one of another. This I say then, Walk in the Spirit, and ye shall not fulfil the lust of the flesh. For the flesh lusteth against the Spirit, and the Spirit against the flesh: and these are contrary the one to the other: so that ye cannot do the things that ye would. But if ye be led of the Spirit, ye are not under the law. Now the works of the flesh are manifest, which are these; Adultery, fornication, uncleanness, lasciviousness, Idolatry, witchcraft, hatred, variance, emulations, wrath, strife, seditions, heresies, Envyings, murders, drunkenness, revellings, and such like: of the which I tell you before, as I have also told you in time past, that they which do such things shall not inherit the kingdom of God. But the fruit of the Spirit is love, joy, peace, longsuffering, gentleness, goodness, faith, Meekness, temperance: against such there is no law. And they that are Christ's have crucified the flesh with the affections and lusts. If we live in the Spirit, let us also walk in the Spirit. Galatians 5:13-25**

The Scriptures make it very clear that those who believe in the Lord Jesus will demonstrate their faith by their obedience to the truth. Jesus is the truth. He is filled with the Spirit of Truth and He came into the world to set us free. Those who do not obey the truth prove that they are not believers and thus have no part in Christ. So, when anyone is presented with the truth and then chooses to go their own way, they are manifesting the spirit of error in the form of rebellion.

71

Dear reader, this is a most important concept for us to understand!

Many are they who call themselves Christians. However, the true evidence of Christian faith for anyone claiming to be a believer is the fruit that is manifested in that person's life. In other words, what we actually observe in a person's speech, attitudes, behavior and lifestyle is what validates that person's claim to be a follower of Jesus.

Let us look into this further and begin by defining two words:

Bondage: The state of one who is bound as a slave or serf; a state of subjection to a force, power or influence.

Rebellion: Open, armed, and organized resistance to a constituted government; an act or a show of defiance toward an authority or established convention.

We learned previously that Jesus came to set us free from bondage to sin. We also learned that when the truth is presented to an individual, that person has the freedom to accept or reject it. Those who accept the truth are believers and immediately set free from this bondage. Those who reject the truth are unbelievers and remain enslaved to sin and to the spirit of error. They are manifesting that spirit in the form of rebellion.

What does Scripture teach us regarding the ability to discern between these two spirits, and what difference will be seen in our lives when we live by one versus the other?

There is therefore now no condemnation to them which are in Christ Jesus, who walk not after the flesh, but after the Spirit. Romans 8:1

If you are relying on a modern translation of the Bible for truth, compare the preceding Scripture with the one in your Bible. You may be shocked to find the second half the verse removed! Now ask yourself, "Why was it removed?" Because it supports the false doctrine of "Once Saved Always Saved", and removes any responsibility on the part of the believer to obey!

For <u>the law of the Spirit of life in Christ Jesus</u> hath made me <u>free</u> from <u>the law of sin and death</u>. For what the law could not do, in that it was <u>weak through the flesh</u>, <u>God sending his own Son</u> in the likeness of sinful flesh, and for sin, condemned sin in the flesh: That the righteousness of the law might be fulfilled in us, <u>who walk not after the flesh, but after the Spirit.</u> For they that are after the flesh do mind the things of the flesh; but they that are after the Spirit the things of the Spirit. For <u>to be carnally minded is death</u>; but <u>to be spiritually minded is life and peace</u>. Because <u>the carnal mind is enmity against God</u>: for it is not subject to the law of God, neither indeed can be. So then <u>they that are in the flesh cannot please God</u>. But ye are not in the flesh, but in the Spirit, <u>if so be that the Spirit of God dwell in you</u>. Now <u>if any man have not the Spirit of Christ, he is none of his</u>. And if Christ be in you, the body is dead because of sin; but the Spirit is life because of righteousness. But if the Spirit of him that raised up Jesus from the dead dwell in you, he that raised up Christ from the dead shall also quicken your mortal bodies by his Spirit that dwelleth in you. Therefore, brethren, we are debtors, not to the flesh, to live after the flesh. For <u>if ye live after the flesh, ye shall die: but if ye through the Spirit do mortify the deeds of the body, ye shall live</u>. <u>For as many as are led by the Spirit of God, they are the sons of God</u>. Romans 8:1-14

So, we see that those who walk after the Spirit of God, which is The Holy Spirit, who is the Spirit of Truth, are those who are the children of God. Conversely, those who walk after the flesh, which is the spirit of error, are the children of disobedience and under the wrath of God.

And you hath he quickened (made alive)**, who were dead in trespasses and sins; Wherein in time past <u>ye walked according to the course of this world</u>, <u>according to the prince of the power of the air</u>, <u>the spirit that now worketh in the children of disobedience</u>: Among whom also <u>we all</u> had our conversation in times past in the lusts of our flesh, fulfilling the desires of the flesh and of the mind; and were <u>by nature the children of wrath</u>, even as others. But God, who is rich in mercy, for his great love wherewith he loved us, Even when we were dead in sins, hath quickened us together with Christ, (by grace ye are saved;) And hath raised us up together, and made us sit together in heavenly places in Christ Jesus: That in the ages to come he might shew the exceeding riches of his grace in his kindness toward us <u>through Christ Jesus</u>. <u>For by grace are ye saved through faith; and that not of yourselves: it is the gift of God</u>: Not of works, lest any man should boast. For we are his workmanship, created in Christ Jesus <u>unto good works</u>, which God hath before ordained <u>that we should walk in them</u>. Ephesians 2:1-10**

Just what does the spirit of error manifesting itself in rebellion look like?

<u>Idolatry</u>: The worship of a created object either made by human hands or created by God instead of, or in addition to, the worship due only to the true God. The term "idol" may also refer to fame, money, power, nationality, ethnicity, or covetousness of anything more than God.

I am the LORD thy God, which have brought thee (you, me, and every other believer) **out of the land of Egypt** (the world)**, out of the house of bondage** (captivity to sin under Satan)**. Thou shalt have no other gods** (not your religion, your house, your car, your career, your bank account, your pleasure, and not YOURSELF) **before me. Exodus 20:1-3**

Witchcraft: The manipulation of others for selfish purposes through the use of spiritual power.

Master, which is the great commandment in the law? Jesus said unto him, Thou shalt love the Lord thy God with all thy heart, and with all thy soul, and with all thy mind. This is the first and great commandment. And the second is like unto it, Thou shalt love thy neighbour as thyself. On these two commandments hang all the law and the prophets. Matthew 26:36-40

Hatred: An emotion of intense revulsion, distaste, or antipathy for a person or thing, generally attributed to a desire to avoid, restrict, remove, or destroy the hated object.

A new commandment I give unto you, That ye love one another; as I have loved you, that ye also love one another. John 13:34

Variance: In a state of dissension or controversy; in a state of enmity.

We are of God: he that knoweth God heareth us; he that is not of God heareth not us. Hereby know we the spirit of truth, and the spirit of error. Beloved, let us love one another: for love is of God; and every one that loveth is born of God, and knoweth

God. He that loveth not knoweth not God; for **God is love**. 1 John 4:6-8

Emulations: a striving to equal or do more than others to obtain carnal favors or honors.

But Jesus called them to him, and saith unto them, Ye know that they which are accounted to rule over the Gentiles exercise lordship over them; and their great ones exercise authority upon them. But so shall it not be among you: but <u>whosoever will be great among you, shall be your minister: And whosoever of you will be the chiefest, shall be servant of all.</u> Mark 10:42-44

Wrath: Violent anger; vehement exasperation; indignation.

And grieve not the holy Spirit of God, whereby ye are sealed unto the day of redemption. Let all bitterness, and wrath, and anger, and clamour, and evil speaking, be put away from you, with all malice: And <u>be ye kind one to another</u>, <u>tenderhearted</u>, <u>forgiving one another</u>, even as God for Christ's sake hath forgiven you. Ephesians 4:30-32

Strife: Exertion or contention for superiority; contest of emulation, either by intellectual or physical efforts.

And he said unto them, The kings of the Gentiles exercise lordship over them; and they that exercise authority upon them are called benefactors. But ye shall not be so: but <u>he that is greatest among you, let him be as the younger; and he that is chief, as he that doth serve</u>. Luke 22:25-26

<u>Sedition</u>: A factious commotion of the people, a tumultuous assembly rising in opposition to law or the administration of justice, and in disturbance of the public peace.

Recompense to no man evil for evil. Provide things honest in the sight of all men. If it be possible, as much as lieth in you, <u>live peaceably with all men</u>. Dearly beloved, <u>avenge not yourselves, but rather give place unto wrath: for it is written, Vengeance is mine; I will repay, saith the Lord</u>. Romans 12:17-19

<u>Heresy</u>: A fundamental error in true doctrine, or an error of opinion respecting some fundamental doctrine of the truth.

But there were <u>false prophets</u> also among the people, even as there shall be <u>false teachers</u> among you, who privily (secretly) shall bring in damnable heresies, <u>even denying the Lord that bought them</u>, and bring upon themselves swift destruction. 2 Peter 2:1

<u>Envying</u>: Ill will at others, on account of some supposed superiority.

Let love be without dissimulation. Abhor that which is evil; cleave to that which is good. Be kindly affectioned one to another with <u>brotherly love</u>; in honour <u>preferring one another</u>; Romans 12:9-10

<u>Murders</u>: The act of unlawfully killing a human being with premeditated malice, by a person of sound mind.

Ye are of your father the devil, and the lusts of your father ye will do. <u>He was a murderer from the beginning</u>, and abode not in the truth, because there is no truth in him. When he

speaketh a lie, he speaketh of his own: for he is a liar, and the father of it. And because I tell you the truth, ye believe me not. John 8:44-45

Drunkenness: Intoxication; inebriation; a state in which a person is overwhelmed or overpowered with spirituous liquors, so that his reason is disordered, and he reels or staggers in walking.

Ye are all the children of light, and the children of the day: we are not of the night, nor of darkness. Therefore let us not sleep, as do others; but <u>let us watch and be sober</u>. For they that sleep sleep in the night; and <u>they that be drunken are drunken in the night</u>. But let us, who are of the day, <u>be sober</u>, putting on the breastplate of faith and love; and for an helmet, the hope of salvation. For <u>God hath not appointed us to wrath, but to obtain salvation by our Lord Jesus Christ</u>, Who died for us, that, whether we wake or sleep, we should live together with him. 1 Thessalonians 5:5-10

Reveling: To feast with loose and clamorous merriment; to carouse; to act the bacchanalian.

Therefore if any man be in Christ, he is a new creature: old things are passed away; behold, all things are become new. 2 Corinthians 5:17

The Spirit of Truth	The spirit of error
Love	Hate - rebellion
Joy	Wrath - rebellion
Peace	Strife - rebellion
Longsuffering (patience)	Sedition - rebellion

78

Gentleness	Murder - rebellion
Goodness	Envying - rebellion
Faith	Heresy - rebellion
Meekness	Emulation - rebellion
Temperance (moderation)	Reveling – rebellion

Our loving God taught us what it is that He requires of us in the opening pages of His word. Through the recorded events in the Scriptures, He progressively reveals the truth to all who have ears to hear. The historical accounts within the written record serve as examples to exhort all of us to obedience through wisdom, and stand as a warning to us of the consequences of disobedience.

Give instruction to a wise man, and he will be yet wiser: teach a just man, and he will increase in learning. <u>The fear of the LORD is the beginning of wisdom</u>: and the knowledge of the holy is understanding. Proverbs 9:9-11

Jesus said:

And I say unto you my friends, Be not afraid of them that kill the body, and after that have no more that they can do. But I will forewarn you whom ye shall fear: Fear him, which after he hath killed hath power to cast into hell; yea, I say unto you, Fear him. Luke 12:4, 5

It becomes readily apparent that the spirit of error, which manifests itself in rebellion, evolves from the concept of idolatry or idol worship. There is no mystery to it, as the spiritual source behind this soul-damning doctrine has been tenaciously active for a long time in the world and is very attractive to the ego in all of us.

Tragically, this spirit has been very successfully promoted over many centuries, leading many deceived souls into hell; this, of course, being the ultimate goal. The author of idolatry has spiritually sired many children of disobedience who have in the past, and are now, <u>living with reckless abandon in all out rebellion against the truth</u>. We have the record of humanity all the way back to the first man and therefore, no excuses for ignorance. Anyone seeking the truth will have no trouble finding it.

For I am not ashamed of the gospel of Christ: for it is the power of God unto <u>salvation to</u> <u>every one that believeth</u>; to the Jew first, and also to the Greek.

For therein is the righteousness of God revealed from faith to faith: as it is written, <u>The just shall live by faith</u>.

For the <u>wrath of God</u> is revealed from heaven <u>against all ungodliness and unrighteousness of men, who hold the truth in unrighteousness</u>;

Because that which may be known of God is manifest in them; for God hath shewed it unto them.

For the invisible things of him from the creation of the world are clearly seen, being understood by the things that are made, even his eternal power and Godhead; <u>so that they are without excuse</u>: Because that, when they knew God, they glorified him not as God, neither were thankful; but <u>became vain in their imaginations, and their foolish heart was darkened. Professing themselves to be wise, they became fools</u>, And changed the glory of the uncorruptible God into an image made like to corruptible man, and to birds, and fourfooted beasts, and creeping things. Wherefore God also <u>gave them up to uncleanness through the lusts of their own hearts, to dishonour</u>

their own bodies between themselves: Who <u>changed the truth of God into a lie, and worshipped</u> and served the creature more than the Creator, who is blessed for ever. Amen. For this cause God gave them up unto <u>vile affections</u>: for even their women did change the natural use into that which is against nature: And likewise also the men, leaving the natural use of the woman, burned in their lust one toward another; men with men working that which is unseemly, and receiving in themselves that recompence of their error which was meet.

(God has made it very clear that He will judge all those who engage in any form of homosexual activity unless they repent. Please do not be deceived by the situational ethics of popular culture. What we see today in society is no different than what Lot saw in Sodom, whose destruction was for our example - 2 Peter 2:6).

And turning the cities of Sodom and Gomorrha into ashes condemned them with an overthrow, making them an ensample unto those that after should live ungodly;) And even as they did not like to retain God in their knowledge, God <u>gave them over to a reprobate mind</u>, to do those things which are not convenient; Being filled with <u>all unrighteousness, fornication, wickedness, covetousness, maliciousness; full of envy, murder, debate, deceit, malignity; whisperers, Backbiters, haters of God, despiteful, proud, boasters, inventors of evil things, disobedient to parents, Without understanding, covenantbreakers, without natural affection, implacable, unmerciful:</u> Who knowing the judgment of God, that <u>they which commit such things are worthy of death</u>, not only do the same, <u>but have pleasure in them that do them</u>. Romans 1:16-31

So, what is this idea, this toxic seed which, when planted into the human heart, is so deadly to the soul? What is this doctrine which the written record in Scripture plainly demonstrates has so successfully and tragically flourished over the course of history?

It is none other than the worship of <u>SELF</u> in all its' variations and permutations.

- self-absorbed
- self-actualization
- self-aggrandizement
- self-appointed
- self-assured
- self-awareness
- self-centered
- self-described
- self-worth
- self-titled
- self-sustaining
- self-serving
- self-willed
- self-taught
- self-styled
- self-rule
- self-righteous
- self-reliant
- self-pity
- self-proclaimed
- self-preservation
- self-possessed
- self-made
- selfish
- self-interest
- self-indulgent
- self-improvement
- self-important
- self-image
- self-help
- self-government
- self-expression
- self-esteem
- self-determination
- self-educated
- self-described
- self-congratulatory
- self-deception

Remember, dear reader, who it was that championed "Self" over everything else and still does through anyone who will receive his soul-damning lies.

How art thou fallen from heaven, O <u>Lucifer</u>, son of the morning! how art thou cut down to the ground, which didst weaken the nations! <u>For thou hast said in thine heart, I will</u> ascend into heaven, <u>I will</u> exalt <u>my</u> throne above the stars of God: <u>I will</u> sit also upon the mount of the congregation, in the sides of the north: <u>I will</u> ascend above the heights of the clouds; <u>I will</u> be like the most High. Yet thou shalt be brought down to hell, to the sides of the pit. Isaiah 14:12-14

Please read the above words again, very carefully. Understanding the context of the words that were said, and who it was that said them, will give any seeker of the truth great insight into why things are the way they are in our world today. Satan, the fallen angel Lucifer, the father of lies, the accuser of the brethren, the deceiver, murderer and destroyer of men's souls, was the first to commit <u>rebellion</u> against God. In doing so, he caused the damnation of a great many other angels, as well as men and women throughout history. Satan is the architect of the spirit of error and its' fruit; <u>rebellion</u>

The story of Cain and Abel gives us great insight into the heart of God and man, as well as the spiritual struggle between truth and error. It is a tragic example of what can happen when we choose to honor ourselves over others. The story reveals very clearly what the spirit of error is and how easily this deadly force can infect the soul of any human.

The story takes place in chapter four of the book of Genesis. It concerns the two sons of Adam and Eve. Abel was a sheep herder and Cain worked the land as a farmer.

And Adam knew Eve his wife; and she conceived, and bare Cain, and said, I have gotten a man from the LORD. And she again bare his brother Abel. And Abel was a keeper of sheep,

83

but Cain was a tiller of the ground. And in process of time it came to pass, that Cain brought of the fruit of the ground an offering unto the LORD. And Abel, he also brought of the firstlings of his flock and of the fat thereof. And the LORD had respect unto Abel and to his offering: But unto Cain and to his offering he had not respect. And <u>Cain was very wroth</u>, and his countenance fell. And the LORD said unto Cain, Why art thou wroth? and why is thy countenance fallen? <u>If thou doest well, shalt thou not be accepted</u>? and <u>if thou doest not well, sin lieth at the door. And unto thee shall be his desire</u>, and thou shalt rule over him. And Cain talked with Abel his brother: and it came to pass, when they were in the field, that Cain rose up against Abel his brother, and slew him. And the LORD said unto Cain, Where is Abel thy brother? And he said, I know not: <u>Am I my brother's keeper</u>? And he said, What hast thou done? the voice of thy brother's blood crieth unto me from the ground. And now art thou cursed from the earth, which hath opened her mouth to receive thy brother's blood from thy hand; When thou tillest the ground, it shall not henceforth yield unto thee her strength; a fugitive and a vagabond shalt thou be in the earth. **Genesis 4:1-12**

After the fall of Adam and Eve through disobedience, God specifically told them that there would be a victory over Satan and sin in the future (for the full account, see Genesis 3).

What was God teaching in this story of Cain and Abel, and where did man fall short? Abel's offering to God was from the first fruits of his flock, while Cain's offering was from the work of his own hands as a farmer. To us, it would seem that Cain's offering might even be superior. After all, he worked hard for the crops that he offered, while Abel merely selected a lamb from his flock. We might think that surely God would value all the effort Cain put into his offering. Why did God accept Abel's and not Cain's offering?

By faith Abel offered unto God **a more excellent sacrifice than Cain**, by which he obtained witness that he was righteous, God testifying of his gifts: and by it he being dead yet speaketh. Hebrews 11:4

We can see the fulfillment of an even better sacrifice than Abel's excellent offering as the New Testament Scriptures tell us:

But ye are come unto mount Sion, and unto the city of the living God, the heavenly Jerusalem, and to an innumerable company of angels, To the general assembly and church of the firstborn, which are written in heaven, and to God the Judge of all, and to the spirits of just men made perfect, And to Jesus the mediator of the new covenant, and to the blood of sprinkling, that speaketh better things than that of Abel. Hebrews 12:22-24

With 20/20 hindsight, we can look back at history and very clearly observe that God was preparing mankind's hearts and minds for the eventual final offering that would be made once and for all. Through the story of Cain and Abel, and many others in the Old Testament, we learn that God is not looking for our prideful accomplishments, but rather a people who have humble hearts. God is far more concerned with the motivations of our hearts than the works of our hands, or the wisdom of our minds. Unlike Cain, Abel did not work for the lamb that he offered God. Able knew that the lamb was created by God and so his offering was made by faith. As all believers learn when they seek God with all their heart, we are saved through faith and not by our own works.

For by grace are ye saved through faith; and that not of yourselves: it is the gift of God: Not of works, lest any man should boast. Ephesians 2:8, 9

As humans, we have always wanted to go our own way; by our own wisdom and in our own strength. In our selfishness, we make up the rules as we define them and as they serve our purposes. The lust of our eyes, the lust of our flesh, and the pride of life have consumed our hearts and resulted in much human tragedy over the course of history. We think like Cain and we look for approval of our work in the fullness of our pride, not realizing that what we are producing is corrupt because our hearts are corrupt. In our rebellion, we create "Religion" to salve our guilt and stroke the vanity of our self-righteousness. With hardened hearts, blind eyes, deaf ears, and vain minds, we ever resist the truth so plainly evident that a child can perceive it.

There is a way <u>which seemeth right</u> unto a man, but the end thereof <u>are the ways of death</u>. Proverbs 14:12

The heart <u>is deceitful above all things</u>, and <u>desperately wicked</u>: who can know it? I the LORD <u>search the heart</u>, I try the reins, even to give every man according to his ways, and according to the fruit of his doings. Jeremiah 17:9, 10

For my thoughts are not your thoughts, neither are your ways my ways, saith the LORD. For as the heavens are higher than the earth, <u>so are my ways higher than your ways</u>, and <u>my thoughts than your thoughts</u>. Isaiah 55:8, 9

Jesus told us that only one who becomes like a little child will enter the Kingdom of Heaven.

Verily I say unto you, Whosoever shall not receive the kingdom of God <u>as a little child</u>, he shall <u>not</u> enter therein. Mark 10:15

Only one who thinks as a child, who is poor in spirit, humble in mind, and pure in heart will be able to hear the truth, receive it, and obey it. In closing, let us read the Scriptures following the one at the start of this chapter:

For in Jesus Christ neither circumcision availeth any thing, nor uncircumcision; but <u>faith which worketh by love</u>. Ye did run well; who did hinder you that ye should not <u>obey the truth</u>? This persuasion cometh not of him that calleth you. A little leaven leaveneth the whole lump. I have confidence in you through the Lord, that ye will be none otherwise minded: but he that troubleth you shall bear his judgment, whosoever he be. And I, brethren, if I yet preach circumcision, why do I yet suffer persecution? <u>then is the offence of the cross ceased</u>. I would they were even cut off which trouble you. For, brethren, ye have been called unto liberty; only <u>use not liberty for an occasion to the flesh</u>, but by love serve one another. For all the law is fulfilled in one word, even in this; <u>Thou shalt love thy neighbour as thyself</u>. Galatians 5:1-14

James, the half-brother of Jesus and leader of the Jerusalem church, puts it very plainly for all of us to understand:

Therefore to him that knoweth to do good, and doeth it not, to him it is sin. James 4:17

Oh Father, I realize that I have no wisdom of my own and I ask You to forgive me for the times that I selfishly went my own way; justifying my actions in the vanity of my thinking. Thank You for granting mercy unto me by giving me time to repent of my wickedness. I love You with all my heart Father and I ask You in the precious name of Jesus to fill me with Your Holy Spirit anew that I might be light and salt to those around me. Amen.

CHAPTER 5

SAVING FAITH AND THE BLESSINGS OF OBEDIENCE

What then? shall we sin, because we are not under the law, but under grace? God forbid. Know ye not, that to whom ye yield yourselves servants to obey, his servants ye are to whom ye obey; whether of sin unto death, or of obedience unto righteousness? Romans 6:15-16

Dear reader, it is imperative that we understand the seriousness of sin. The most critical information needed for the well-being of our souls is the knowledge of the truth regarding iniquity and unrighteousness. Sinning will cause us to be separated from a Holy God and, if we do not repent, will result in our eternal damnation in the lake of fire. This truth revealed by God is so important for us to comprehend that I am compelled to state the warning very clearly. My heart is especially burdened for our younger men and women who have not heard the truth. The prince of this world has been working very hard to blind the eyes of those who might otherwise see and be saved. He does this through the "Spirit of error" and he has successfully deceived many who, after death (and to their own horror), have found themselves in a terrifying furnace of fire from which there is no escape.

The greatest tragedy of disobedience to our Creator and Holy God was the fall of man in the Garden of Eden. The greatest blessing of obedience is eternal life, which comes to us through the obedience of the ONLY one who can save - Jesus. This is where faith comes in to the picture.

If there is one question that every professing believer in Jesus Christ should be able to answer it must be, "what is faith?" Understanding what faith is, and is not, is of utmost importance to the welfare of our souls. Anyone who is hungering and thirsting for the truth will want to know the answer to this question, as well as how it applies to their life in this world. Let us look into the Holy Scriptures to learn the truth regarding this most essential doctrine. What follows are seven questions to help us identify "Saving Faith" and be certain that we have it. As believers, the apostle Paul warns us not to be complacent, but to take an active role in maintaining our relationship with Jesus.

Examine yourselves, whether ye be in the faith; prove your own selves. Know ye not your own selves, how that Jesus Christ is in you, except ye be reprobates? 2 Corinthians 13:5

What is Faith?

Today, if you ask any one of ten people you encountered on the streets of America whether or not they are a Christian, the majority would say that they indeed are. Incredibly though, if you follow up with the question "What is a Christian?", many would be hard pressed to answer you, would not be able to explain the Gospel (good news) of Jesus, nor would they be able to define what faith in Christ means.

Now faith is <u>the substance of things hoped for</u>, <u>the evidence of things not seen</u>. For by it the elders obtained a good report. Through faith we understand that the worlds were framed by the word of God, so that things which are seen were not made of things which do appear. Hebrews 11:1-3

It used to be a well-known fact that America was founded on Christian principles and that the men who established our country were devout Christians. Today, many well-known individuals, as well as the producers of mass media, would have us believe that this is not true and that it is wrong to acknowledge God, or His only begotten Son, Jesus. As far as they are concerned, there is no supreme creator and it is just not "Politically correct" to say otherwise.

Our Lord Himself gave us the reason why:

He that believeth on him is not condemned: but <u>he that believeth not is condemned already, because he hath not believed in the name of the only begotten Son of God.</u> And this is the condemnation, that light is come into the world, and <u>men loved darkness rather than light, because their deeds were evil.</u> For every one that doeth evil hateth the light, neither cometh to the light, lest his deeds should be reproved. John 3:18-20

Faith is a relationship, not a religion. It is a covenant of love between a created being, which is any one of us, and Jesus, the Son of God. Religion is a set of external rituals, ordinances, sacraments and laws. Faith is an internal commitment of the heart to the One, Jesus, who represents the fullness of the wisdom of God. He is the One and only One who provides reconciliation between fallen mankind and the Father.

For I would that ye knew what great conflict I have for you, and for them at Laodicea, and for as many as have not seen my face in the flesh; That their hearts might be comforted, being knit together in love, and unto all riches of the full assurance of understanding, to the acknowledgement of the mystery of God, and of the Father, and of Christ; <u>In whom are hid all the treasures of wisdom and knowledge.</u> Colossians 2:1-3

90

Why is faith so important?

The following Scripture speaks volumes:

But <u>without faith it is impossible to please him</u>: for he that cometh to God <u>must believe that he is, and that he is a rewarder of them that diligently seek him</u>. Hebrews 11:6

Where does faith come from?

This is a very good question. Where does a person find faith? Where can one learn about faith? Thankfully, our most merciful and loving God has provided us with the answers in His written word. The Bible is the source of understanding for all questions regarding faith and Scriptures clearly tell us who the author is.

So then <u>faith cometh by hearing, and hearing by the word of God</u>. Romans 10:17

Wherefore seeing we also are compassed about with so great a cloud of witnesses, let us lay aside every weight, and the sin which doth so easily beset us, and let us run with patience the race that is set before us, <u>Looking unto Jesus the author and finisher of our faith</u>; who for the joy that was set before him endured the cross, despising the shame, and is set down at the right hand of the throne of God. For consider him that endured such contradiction of sinners against himself, lest ye be wearied and faint in your minds. Hebrews 12:1-3

For the Son of man is come to seek and to save that which was lost. Luke 19:10

Who is the object of our faith?

The object of our faith is the One who has paid the debt that we rightly owe.

For ye are all the children of God by <u>faith in Christ Jesus</u>. Galatians 3:26

For this cause I bow my knees unto the Father of our Lord Jesus Christ, Of whom the whole family in heaven and earth is named, That he would grant you, according to the riches of his glory, to be strengthened with might by his Spirit in the inner man; <u>That Christ may dwell in your hearts by faith</u>; that ye, being rooted and grounded in love, May be able to comprehend with all saints what is the breadth, and length, and depth, and height; And to know the love of Christ, which passeth knowledge, that ye might be filled with all the fulness of God. Ephesians 3:14-19

We give thanks to God and the Father of our Lord Jesus Christ, praying always for you, Since we heard of your <u>faith in Christ Jesus</u>, and of the love which ye have to all the saints, For the hope which is laid up for you in heaven, whereof ye heard before in the word of the truth of the gospel; Colossians 1:3-5

And that from a child thou hast known the holy scriptures, <u>which are able to make thee wise unto salvation through faith which is in Christ Jesus</u>. 2 Timothy 3:15

What are we to do with our faith?

Dear reader, we must not deceive ourselves. Saving faith is a living faith. It is a visible faith that can be plainly observed in our good works. It is obedient to the truth and is ultimately expressed by love toward others as we live our new lives in Christ knowing that God expressed His highest love toward us in the gift of His own

Son. We must assuredly beyond a shadow of doubt, understand that saving faith will be reflected in a radically different lifestyle from our past. The first thing we must do with our faith is add to it.

The apostle Peter gives us an excellent road map for us as we live by faith in this world:

Simon Peter, a servant and an apostle of Jesus Christ, to them that have obtained like precious faith with us through the righteousness of God and our Saviour Jesus Christ: Grace and peace be multiplied unto you through the knowledge of God, and of Jesus our Lord, According as his divine power hath given unto us all things that pertain unto life and godliness, through the knowledge of him that hath called us to glory and virtue: Whereby are given unto us exceeding great and precious promises: <u>that by these ye might be partakers of the divine nature, having escaped the corruption that is in the world through lust</u>. And beside this, <u>giving all diligence, add to your faith virtue</u>; <u>and to virtue knowledge</u>; <u>And to knowledge temperance</u>; <u>and to temperance patience</u>; <u>and to patience godliness</u>; <u>And to godliness brotherly kindness</u>; <u>and to brotherly kindness charity</u>. 2 Peter 1:1-7

We are wise if we add to our faith virtue, knowledge, temperance, patience, godliness, brotherly kindness, and ultimately charity. Additionally, we are to do many other things with our faith in Christ (I encourage you to look up the Scripture references for you own edification). We are to:

- Continue in it (Acts 14:22, Col. 1:23, 1 Tim. 2:15)

- Live by it (Rom. 1:17, Gal. 2:20)

- Stand by it (Rom. 11:20)

- Obey it (Rom. 16:16)

- Walk by it (2 Cor. 5:7)

- Examine ourselves to see if we are in it (2 Cor. 13:5)

- Fight the good fight with it (1 Tim. 6:12)

- Keep it (1 Tim. 4:7)

- Prove it by our works (James 2:18)

- Earnestly contend for it (Jude 1:3)

What does our faith do for us?

Peter goes on to tell us of the many blessings of obedience that our faith will do for us. Primarily, we will have assurance of our salvation within our hearts and bear much good fruit for the Kingdom of God. Continuing the Scripture above:

For if these things be in you, and abound, they make you that <u>ye shall neither be barren</u> <u>nor unfruitful</u> in the knowledge of our Lord Jesus Christ. But he that lacketh these things is blind, and cannot see afar off, and hath forgotten that he was purged from his old sins. Wherefore the rather, brethren, <u>give diligence to make your calling and election sure</u>: <u>for if ye do these things, ye shall never fall</u>: <u>For so an entrance shall be ministered unto you abundantly into the everlasting kingdom of our Lord and Saviour Jesus Christ</u>. Wherefore I will not be negligent to put you always in remembrance of these things,

**though ye know them, and <u>be established in the present truth</u>.
2 Peter 1:8-12**

There are MANY other wonderful blessings and promises that our
faith in Jesus will do for us. A living faith which saves:

- Purifies our hearts (Acts 15:9)

- Sanctifies us (Acts 26:187)

- Makes us righteous (Rom. 3:22, 25; Phil. 3:9)

- Justifies us (Rom. 3:28, 5:1; Gal. 2:16, 3:24)

- Gives us peace with God (Rom. 5:1)

- Causes us to be blessed (Gal. 3:9)

- By it we receive the promise of the Spirit (Gal. 3:14)

- Saves us (Eph. 2:8)

- Gives us joy (Phil. 1:25)

- Protects us from enemies (Eph. 6:16)

- Works patience in us (James 1:3)

Finally, what is the end result of our faith?

The Apostle Peter tells us with these precious words of wisdom:

**Blessed be the God and Father of our Lord Jesus Christ, which
according to his abundant mercy <u>hath begotten us again unto a</u>**

lively hope by the resurrection of Jesus Christ from the dead, To an inheritance incorruptible, and undefiled, and that fadeth not away, reserved in heaven for you, Who are kept by the power of God through faith unto salvation ready to be revealed in the last time. Wherein ye greatly rejoice, though now for a season, if need be, ye are in heaviness through manifold temptations: That the trial of **your faith, being much more precious than of gold** that perisheth, though it be tried with fire, might be found unto praise and honour and glory at the appearing of Jesus Christ: Whom having not seen, ye love; in whom, though now ye see him not, yet believing, ye rejoice with joy unspeakable and full of glory: **Receiving the end of your faith, even the salvation of your souls**. 1 Peter 1:3-9

Now, I want to put in your minds the conclusion of the matter regarding saving faith, so that there will be no misunderstanding. It is so critically important, dear reader, that you understand the following:

The end of our faith is the salvation of our souls. Let us not be deceived. If we have faith, we believe. If we believe, we obey the truth. If we do not obey, we do not have faith and that makes us unbelievers. If we do not repent, our destination is eternal torment in the lake of fire.

But the fearful, and unbelieving, and the abominable, and murderers, and whoremongers, and sorcerers, and idolaters, and all liars, shall have their part in the lake which burneth with fire and brimstone: which is the second death Revelation 21:8.

This leads me to expose a pernicious false doctrine that has run rampant in Christian circles for some time now. The idea that a person can make a one-time decision to "Accept Christ" and then

96

never lose their salvation, regardless of the way they live the rest of their lives, is known as the doctrine of unconditional eternal security, otherwise known as "Once Saved Always Saved – OSAS".

To begin with, let us define the word, "Pernicious":

Having a harmful effect, especially in a gradual or subtle way; causing insidious harm or ruin; injurious; hurtful; deadly; fatal; evil; wicked; tending to cause death or serious injury; causing great harm; destructive.

This is a very accurate description of the nature and effect of this extremely deceptive false doctrine. Why is this doctrine so dangerous?

- It removes the fear of God from the heart.

  By mercy and truth iniquity is purged: and by the fear of the Lord men depart from evil. Proverbs 16:6

- It removes the requirement for obedience to the truth.

  To them who by patient continuance in well doing seek for glory and honour and immortality, eternal life: But unto them that are contentious, and do not obey the truth, but obey unrighteousness, indignation and wrath, Romans 2:7, 8

- It allows a continued sinful lifestyle, with no consequences.

  Nevertheless the foundation of God standeth sure, having this seal, The Lord knoweth them that are his.

And, let every one that nameth the name of Christ depart from iniquity. 2 Timothy 2:19

- It provides a road to salvation which is in reality a road to damnation.

  Marvel not at this: for the hour is coming, in the which all that are in the graves shall hear his voice, And shall come forth; they that have done good, unto the resurrection of life; and they that have done evil, unto the resurrection of damnation. John 5:28, 29

Several years ago, I was involved in a discussion regarding the doctrine of "Once Saved Always Saved" with another brother in Christ. He was adamantly in favor of this doctrine and believed it to be the truth. Dear reader, as believers we have many enemies of the cross of Christ. Principal among them, are the following four:

- The World – Friendship with the world is enmity with God (James 4:4)

- The Devil – Our adversary, as a roaring lion, seeks whom he may devour (1 Peter 5:8)

- Our Flesh – Wars against the spirit (Galatians 5:17)

- Our Mind – Our own vanity blinds us to the truth (Romans 1:20-22)

Anyone of these enemies can be very effective in leading us away from the truth. In the case if my brother, I believe he had built up the idea of unconditional eternal security in his own mind based on what he had heard from others. This is a very dangerous thing to do when our very souls are at stake.

98

For though we walk in the flesh, we do not war after the flesh: (For the weapons of our warfare are not carnal, but mighty through God to the pulling down of strong holds;) Casting down imaginations, and every high thing that exalteth itself against the knowledge of God, and <u>bringing into captivity every thought to the obedience of Christ</u>; And having in a readiness to revenge all disobedience, when your obedience is fulfilled. 2 Corinthians 10:3-6

So, in our discussion, I asked him to read all the words of Jesus in the book of Matthew (red in some Bibles) and see if he still believed in once saved always saved when finished. Had he done what I asked, he would have read these words that Jesus spoke:

Ye are the salt of the earth: but <u>if the salt have lost his savour,</u> wherewith shall it be salted? it is thenceforth good for nothing, but to be cast out, and to be trodden under foot of men. Matthew 5:13

In this quote, Jesus is talking to His disciples – believers.

But I say unto you, That whosoever looketh on a woman to lust after her hath committed adultery with her already in his heart. And <u>if thy right eye offend thee</u>, pluck it out, and cast it from thee: for it is profitable for thee that one of thy members should perish, and not that thy whole body should be cast into hell. Matthew 5:28, 29

Jesus is talking to believers. This warning is very important for all those ensnared by internet pornography.

And <u>if thy right hand offend thee</u>, cut it off, and cast it from thee: for it is profitable for thee that one of thy members

should perish, and not that thy whole body should be cast into hell. Matthew 5:30

Again, Jesus is speaking to believers. We are responsible for our actions.

Not every one that saith unto me, Lord, Lord, shall enter into the kingdom of heaven; but <u>he that doeth the will of my Father</u> which is in heaven. Matthew 7:21

Jesus is still talking to believers, or those who think they are. He makes a very clear statement as to what is required of anyone professing to be one of His followers.

And many false prophets shall rise, and shall deceive many. And because iniquity shall abound, <u>the love of many shall wax cold</u>. <u>But he that shall endure unto the end</u>, the same shall be saved. Matthew 7:11-13

Enduring to the end means one started the race, i.e. a believer. Many believers will let their love for Jesus grow cold.

Who then is a <u>faithful and wise servant</u>, whom his lord hath made ruler over his household, to give them meat in due season? Blessed is that servant, whom his lord when he cometh shall find so doing. Verily I say unto you, That he shall make him ruler over all his goods. But and <u>if</u> that evil servant shall say in his heart, My lord delayeth his coming; And shall begin to smite his fellowservants, and to eat and drink with the drunken;The lord of that servant shall come in a day when he looketh not for him, and in an hour that he is not aware of, And <u>shall cut him asunder, and appoint him his portion with the hypocrites</u>: there shall be weeping and gnashing of teeth. Matthew 24:45-51

A servant is a believer.

Then he which had received the one talent came and said, Lord, I knew thee that thou art an hard man, reaping where thou hast not sown, and gathering where thou hast not strawed: And I was afraid, and went and hid thy talent in the earth: lo, there thou hast that is thine. His lord answered and said unto him, <u>Thou wicked and slothful servant</u>, thou knewest that I reap where I sowed not, and gather where I have not strawed: Thou oughtest therefore to have put my money to the exchangers, and then at my coming I should have received mine own with usury. Take therefore the talent from him, and give it unto him which hath ten talents. For unto every one that hath shall be given, and he shall have abundance: but from him that hath not shall be taken away even that which he hath. And <u>cast ye the unprofitable servant into outer darkness</u>: there shall be weeping and gnashing of teeth. Matthew 25:24-30

For anyone claiming to be a Christian, there should be no misunderstanding as to what Jesus requires of us in our walk with Him through this life. To imagine that we can hear the words of faith spoken from the Bible – the written Word of God, say we believe the Gospel of Jesus, make a public profession of faith, be baptized into the body of Christ, and then continue on in our old life just as before is gross self-deception. Furthermore, to make light of sin after knowing what it cost Jesus to pay the debt we owe for our transgressions is to make a mockery of a Holy God; the One who will call all men to account at the judgment. We must realize that to live this way while claiming to be a Christian is nothing less than Laodicean cheap grace. It destroys one's testimony of the truth, weakens the faith of the gullible, provides excuses for the unbelieving world to deny Jesus, and is an act of direct rebellion against the gift of the Savior that we, who are guilty and so undeserving, have been given by God.

Now the parable is this: The seed is the word of God. Those by the way side are they that hear; then cometh the devil, and taketh away the word out of their hearts, lest they should believe and be saved. <u>They on the rock are they, which, when they hear, receive the word with joy; and these have no root, which for a while believe, and in time of temptation fall away.</u> And that which fell among thorns are they, which, when they have heard, go forth, and are choked with cares and riches and pleasures of this life, and bring no fruit to perfection. But that on the good ground are they, which in an honest and good heart, having heard the word, keep it, and bring forth fruit with patience. Luke 8:11-15

The seeds on the rock are believers who fell away. They began as true believers.

For what is a man advantaged, if he gain the whole world, and lose himself, <u>or be cast away</u>? Luke 9:25

In order to be cast away, one must be on the ship in the first place, i.e. a believer.

And Jesus said unto him, No man, having put his hand to the plough, and looking back, is fit for the kingdom of God. Luke 9:62

Once we have escaped the world through freedom in Christ, we must not look back. Jesus said to remember Lot's wife as a warning to all of us to press on in the faith.

Then Peter said unto him, Lord, speakest thou this parable unto us, or even to all? And the Lord said, Who then is that <u>faithful and wise steward</u>, whom his lord shall make ruler over his household, to give them their portion of meat in due

season? Blessed is that <u>servant</u>, whom his lord when he cometh shall find so doing. Of a truth I say unto you, that he will make him ruler over all that he hath. But and if that <u>servant</u> say in his heart, <u>My lord</u> delayeth his coming; and shall begin to beat the menservants and maidens, and to eat and drink, and to be drunken; The lord of that <u>servant</u> will come in a day when he looketh not for him, and at an hour when he is not aware, and will cut him in sunder, and <u>will appoint him his portion with the unbelievers</u>. And that <u>servant</u>, which knew his lord's will, and prepared not himself, neither did according to his will, shall be beaten with many stripes. But he that knew not, and did commit things worthy of stripes, shall be beaten with few stripes. For unto whomsoever much is given, of him shall be much required: and to whom men have committed much, of him they will ask the more. Luke 12:41-48

It is very clear that Jesus is talking about His followers, i.e. believers. He even makes a distinction between the wicked servant and the unbelievers. This teaching makes it very clear that we must watch and pray, and obey lest we fall into temptation.

I am the true vine, and my Father is the husbandman. <u>Every branch in me that beareth not fruit he taketh away</u>: and every branch that beareth fruit, he purgeth it, that it may bring forth more fruit. Now ye are clean through the word which I have spoken unto you. Abide in me, and I in you. As the branch cannot bear fruit of itself, except it abide in the vine; no more can ye, except ye abide in me. I am the vine, ye are the branches: He that abideth in me, and I in him, the same bringeth forth much fruit: for without me ye can do nothing. <u>If a man abide not in me, he is cast forth as a branch, and is withered; and men gather them, and cast them into the fire, and they are burned.</u> If ye abide in me, and my words abide in you, ye shall ask what ye will, and it shall be done unto you.

Herein is my Father glorified, that ye bear much fruit; so shall ye be my disciples. As the Father hath loved me, so have I loved you: continue ye in my love. <u>If ye keep my commandments, ye shall abide in my love</u>; even as I have kept my Father's commandments, and abide in his love. John 15:1-10

The false doctrine of unconditional eternal security or "Once Saved Always Saved" is emphatically rebuked and clearly exposed as false by the above words of Jesus. As believers, we cannot possibly read the preceding Scripture and conclude that we have no responsibility as to how we live our lives.

A man who knew well the difference between <u>cheap grace</u> and <u>costly grace</u> had this to say (underlines my emphasis):

> "<u>Cheap grace is the deadly enemy of our Church</u>. We are fighting today for costly grace. Cheap grace means grace sold on the market like cheapjack's wares. The sacraments, the forgiveness of sin, and the consolations of religion are thrown away at cut prices. Grace is represented as the Church's inexhaustible treasury, from which she showers blessings with generous hands, without asking questions or fixing limits. Grace without price; grace without cost! The essence of grace, we suppose, is that the account has been paid in advance; and, because it has been paid, everything can be had for nothing....
>
> <u>Cheap grace means grace as a doctrine, a principle, a system</u>. It means forgiveness of sins proclaimed as a general truth, the love of God taught as the Christian 'conception' of God. An intellectual assent to that idea is held to be of itself sufficient to secure remission of sins.... In such a Church the world finds a cheap covering for its

sins; no contrition is required, still less any real desire to be delivered from sin. Cheap grace therefore amounts to a denial of the living Word of God, in fact, a denial of the Incarnation of the Word of God.

Cheap grace means the justification of sin without the justification of the sinner. Grace alone does everything they say, and so everything can remain as it was before. *'All for sin could not atone.'* Well, then, let the Christian live like the rest of the world, let him model himself on the world's standards in every sphere of life, and not presumptuously aspire to live a different life under grace from his old life under sin....

Cheap grace is the grace we bestow on ourselves. Cheap grace is the preaching of forgiveness without requiring repentance, baptism without church discipline, Communion without confession.... Cheap grace is grace without discipleship, grace without the cross, grace without Jesus Christ, living and incarnate.

Costly grace is the treasure hidden in the field; for the sake of it a man' will gladly go and sell all that he has. It is the pearl of great price to buy which the merchant will sell all his goods. It is the kingly rule of Christ, for whose sake a man will pluck out the eye which causes him to stumble, it is the call of Jesus Christ at which the disciple leaves his nets and follows him.

Costly grace is the gospel which must be sought again and again and again, the gift which must be asked for, the door at which a man must knock. Such grace is costly because it calls us to follow, and it is grace because it calls us to follow Jesus Christ. It is costly because it costs a man his life, and it is grace because it gives a man the only true life. It is costly because it condemns sin and grace because it justifies the sinner. Above all, it is costly because it cost God the life of his Son: "ye were bought at a price," and what has cost God much cannot be cheap for us. Above all, it is grace because God did not reckon his Son too dear a price to pay for our life, but delivered him up for us. Costly grace is the Incarnation of God.

Costly grace is the sanctuary of God; it has to be protected from the world, and not thrown to the dogs. It is therefore the living word, the Word of God, which he speaks as it pleases him. Costly grace confronts us as a gracious call to follow Jesus. It comes as a word of forgiveness to the broken spirit and the contrite heart. Grace is costly because it compels a man to submit to the yoke of Christ and follow him; it is grace because Jesus says: "My yoke is easy and my burden is light." – Dietrich Bonhoeffer, *The Cost of Discipleship*

This man knew the difference between cheap grace and costly grace. He was a living testimony to the truth and sealed it with his own blood. He was one of the few who stood up against the despicable evil of Adolph Hitler's NAZI regime and, on April 9th, 1945, was executed by special order of Himmler at the Flossenburg concentration camp, just a few days before it was liberated by the Allies.

Now we are in a better position to understand what the Scriptures tell us about the importance of obedience.

Behold, I set before you this day <u>a blessing</u> and <u>a curse</u>; <u>A blessing, if ye obey the commandments of the Lord your God</u>, which I command you this day: And <u>a curse, if ye will not obey</u>

the commandments of the Lord your God, but turn aside out of the way which I command you this day, to go after other gods, which ye have not known. Deuteronomy 11:26-28

The Scriptures were written for our understanding and example. God does not change. He is the Great I AM. He is eternal and His requirements of us remain the same. We all have a choice to either obey the truth or rebel against it and follow our own way. Our attitudes, motivations and actions will all have consequences for us; in this world and the next.

Though he were a Son, yet learned he obedience by the things which he suffered; And being made perfect, he became the author of eternal salvation unto all them that obey him; Hebrews 5:8, 9

Our example is Jesus, the One who obeyed the Father. We, who call ourselves believers, are to do likewise. Dear reader, this is the narrow road. This is the road that not many find, but it is the one filled with many great and precious promises, as well as the one that leads to eternal life. This is the road that those who are seeking the Lord with all their heart will eventually come to. The sign post at the start of this road can be clearly seen by those who have come to the end of themselves. It is the cross of Jesus Christ. It is the beginning of the way of life.

Enter ye in at the strait (narrow) **gate: for wide is the gate, and broad is the way, that leadeth to destruction, and many there be which go in thereat: Because strait** (narrow) **is the gate, and narrow is the way, which leadeth unto life, and few there be that find it. Matthew 7:13-14**

Then said Jesus unto his disciples, If any man will come after me, let him deny himself, and take up his cross, and follow me.

For whosoever will save his life shall lose it: and whosoever will lose his life for my sake shall find it. For what is a man profited, if he shall gain the whole world, and lose his own soul? or what shall a man give in exchange for his soul? Matthew 16:24-26

If we, through faith in Jesus, obey him, then the many blessings of obedience will be granted to us by the Holy Spirit He gives to us.

Then Peter and the other apostles answered and said, We ought to obey God rather than men. The God of our fathers raised up Jesus, whom ye slew and hanged on a tree. Him hath God exalted with his right hand to be a Prince and a Saviour, for to give repentance to Israel, and forgiveness of sins. And we are his witnesses of these things; and so is also the Holy Ghost, whom God hath given to them that obey him. Acts 5:29-32

Peter tells us that the blessing of obedience is the gift of the Holy Ghost!

But we are sure that the judgment of God is according to truth against them which commit such things. And thinkest thou this, O man, that judgest them which do such things, and doest the same, that thou shalt escape the judgment of God? Or despisest thou the riches of his goodness and forbearance and longsuffering; not knowing that the goodness of God leadeth thee to repentance? But after thy hardness and impenitent heart treasurest up unto thyself wrath against the day of wrath and revelation of the righteous judgment of God; Who will render to every man according to his deeds: To them who by patient continuance in well doing seek for glory and honour and immortality, eternal life: But unto them that are contentious, and do not obey the truth, but obey unrighteousness, indignation and wrath Tribulation and

anguish, upon every soul of man that doeth evil, of the Jew first, and also of the Gentile; But glory, honour, and peace, to every man that worketh good, to the Jew first, and also to the Gentile: <u>For there is no respect of persons with God</u>. Romans 2:2-11

The apostle Paul tells us that the blessing of obedience is <u>eternal life</u>!

He also warns us what the eternal consequences will be for disobedience.

Remember dear reader, our good works do NOT save us. Our good works are the evidence to the world that we ARE saved. If we say that we believe and do not do what we say we believe, then we are hypocrites, deceived and lost. If we love one another as Jesus loves us, then we will fulfill the law and the prophets by the visible evidence of saving faith and thus be known as children of God. Please read the following Scripture carefully. It contains the full counsel of God regarding His purpose for us.

And you hath he quickened (made alive), **who were dead in trespasses and sins; Wherein in time past ye walked according to the course of this world, <u>according to the prince of the power of the air, the spirit that now worketh in the children of disobedience</u>: Among whom also <u>we all</u> had our conversation in times past <u>in the lusts of our flesh</u>, fulfilling the desires <u>of the flesh</u> and <u>of the mind</u>; and were <u>by nature the children of wrath</u>, even as others. But God, who is rich in mercy, for his great love wherewith he loved us, Even when we were dead in sins, hath quickened** (made alive) **us together with Christ, <u>(by grace ye are saved)</u> And hath raised us up together, and made us sit together in heavenly places in Christ Jesus: That <u>in the ages to come he might shew the exceeding riches of his grace in</u>**

his kindness toward us through Christ Jesus. For by grace are ye saved through faith; and that not of yourselves: it is the gift of God: Not of works, lest any man should boast. For we are his workmanship, **created in Christ Jesus unto good works,** which God hath before ordained that **we should walk in them.** Ephesians 2:1-10

Through obedience, our lives will be filled with the fruit of the Holy Spirit; love, joy, peace, long suffering, goodness, gentleness, faith, meekness and temperance. We will be children of God and salt and light in a decaying and dark world. We will have a living hope in our hearts that, one day, we will be redeemed from our mortal bodies to inherit eternal life with our Lord and King. We will receive all the great and precious promises of our God, reserved for all those who receive His amazing grace and will accept it by obeying the truth.

For if we sin wilfully after that we have received the knowledge of the truth, there remaineth no more sacrifice for sins, But a certain fearful looking for of judgment and fiery indignation, which shall devour the adversaries. He that despised Moses' law died without mercy under two or three witnesses: Of how much sorer punishment, suppose ye, shall he be thought worthy, who hath trodden under foot the Son of God, and hath counted the blood of the covenant, wherewith he was sanctified, an unholy thing, and hath done despite unto the Spirit of grace? For we know him that hath said, Vengeance belongeth unto me, I will recompense, saith the Lord. And again, The Lord shall judge his people. It is a fearful thing to fall into the hands of the living God. Hebrews 10:26-31

Our lives were bought at a supreme cost to a Holy God and we must not lose sight of what it cost Him!

Wherefore gird up the loins of your mind, be sober, and hope to the end for the grace that is to be brought unto you at the revelation of Jesus Christ; <u>As obedient children</u>, not fashioning yourselves according to the former lusts in your ignorance: But as he which hath called you is holy, so be ye holy in all manner of conversation; Because it is written, Be ye holy; for I am holy. And if ye call on the Father, who without respect of persons judgeth according to every man's work, pass the time of your sojourning here in fear: Forasmuch as ye know that ye were not redeemed with corruptible things, as silver and gold, from your vain conversation received by tradition from your fathers; But with the precious blood of Christ, as of a lamb without blemish and without spot: Who verily was foreordained before the foundation of the world, but was manifest in these last times for you, Who by him do believe in God, that raised him up from the dead, and gave him glory; that your faith and hope might be in God. Seeing <u>ye have purified your souls in obeying the truth</u> through the Spirit unto unfeigned love of the brethren, see that <u>ye love one another with a pure heart fervently</u>: <u>Being born again</u>, not of corruptible seed, but of incorruptible, by <u>the word of God</u>, which <u>liveth and abideth for ever</u>. 1 Peter 1:13-23

In closing this chapter, I submit for your earnest consideration, dear reader, a quote from Donald Stamps, the editor of The Life in the Spirit Study Bible. I highly recommend this resource for all believers seeking a deeper relationship with Jesus.

"The earliest creed or confession of the New Testament church was not Jesus is Savior, but Jesus is Lord (Rom. 10:9; Acts 8:16, 19:5; 1 Cor. 12:3). Jesus Christ is specifically called Savior 16 times in the New Testament and Lord more than 450 times. The current teaching in some evangelical circles that Jesus can be one's Savior without necessarily being one's Lord is found nowhere in the New Testament. No one can receive Jesus as Savior without receiving Him as Lord. This is an essential ingredient in apostolic preaching (Acts 36:40)." Donald Stamps, *Life in the Spirit Study Bible*

My heavenly Father and Most High and Holy One, I come to You in all humility to confess my sins that I offended You with in the past. Please forgive me for all the times I treated Your amazing grace and salvation lightly, and for the times that I did not consider the horrifically brutal death of Your precious Son, Jesus, whom You sent to pay the price for my iniquities. Please forgive me for the times I made light of sin in my life and the times I walked with a lukewarm heart before You. Jesus, be my Lord this day and for all the days I am given to live. Father, I love You with all my heart, soul, mind, and strength and I will obey the truth. Please fill me with Your Holy Spirit today and grant me a heart like Jesus. In His glorious name I pray, amen.

Chapter 6

THE POWER OF CHRIST IN YOU

I can do all things through Christ which strengtheneth me.
Philippians 4:13

In the preceding chapter, we learned that saving faith is a living faith which is visible and not hidden. In other words, true faith will be plainly observable in our lives as a result of our obedience to the commands of Jesus. To be sure, the good works that we do as believers are actually the good works that He does through us as we yield our hearts and lives to Him. We do this because we believe the Gospel of Jesus Christ. Dear reader, this is a very important truth for us to remember as we walk with Jesus day-to-day throughout our lives. Many believers, including myself, can recount the early days of faith in Jesus when, as new born again Christians, we were on fire to change the world for our Lord. As time went on though, we found the struggle to be holy, pure, and obedient growing more difficult. We stumbled and failed in areas that we thought we had already conquered. We became disheartened as we soon discovered that we were totally inadequate to follow Christ in our own strength. We had so carelessly forgotten the clear words of Jesus:

I am the vine, ye are the branches: <u>He that abideth in me, and I in him, the same bringeth forth much fruit</u>: for <u>without me ye can do nothing</u>. John 15:5

Beloved saints, when we put our trust in Jesus we are beginning an awesome love relationship with the One who has conquered sin, death, the world, and Satan! We are surrendering our lives to the One whose name is above all names, the King of kings, the Lord of lords, the One who holds ALL power and authority in Heaven and Earth. The final words of Jesus to His disciples before ascending into Heaven give us great hope and confidence in our Savior and our future if we choose to remain in the faith.

And Jesus came and spake unto them, saying, <u>All power</u> is given unto me in heaven and in earth. Go ye therefore, and teach all nations, baptizing them in the name of the Father, and of the Son, and of the Holy Ghost: Teaching them to observe all things whatsoever I have commanded you: and, lo, I am with you always, even unto the end of the world. Amen. Matthew 28:18-20

If we know this truth, then we should not be surprised when we fail in our own efforts to be holy. Eventually, we will realize that our Lord graciously allows us to fail in order for us to learn the lesson that is so hard for many of us to grasp. The reason it is so difficult for us to comprehend is that, before we can begin to be a branch, we have to stop trying to be the vine. We are not the vine. Jesus is the vine. Until we make an active decision to come to the end of ourselves, we will always be our own worst enemy in bearing good fruit for God and we will utterly fail in our attempts to live a holy life. We must understand that we cannot follow Jesus in our own perceived wisdom. Additionally, we must not negotiate with our flesh for the same reason that we do not negotiate with the devil, the world, or the vain thoughts in our minds. That road is the one paved with good intentions that, with all deceptiveness, leads us straight to hell.

Jesus told us what we must do:

Verily, verily, I say unto you, Except a corn of wheat fall into the ground and die, it abideth alone: <u>but if it die, it bringeth forth much fruit. He that loveth his life shall lose it; and he that hateth his life in this world shall keep it unto life eternal.</u> If any man serve me, let him follow me; and where I am, there shall also my servant be: if any man serve me, him will my Father honour. John 12:24-26

Even the apostle Paul had to learn this critical lesson.

And lest I should be exalted above measure through the abundance of the revelations, there was given to me a thorn in the flesh, the messenger of Satan to buffet me, lest I should be exalted above measure. For this thing I besought the Lord thrice, that it might depart from me. And he said unto me, <u>My grace is sufficient for thee: for my strength is made perfect in weakness.</u> Most gladly therefore will I rather glory in my infirmities, that the power of Christ may rest upon me. Therefore I take pleasure in infirmities, in reproaches, in necessities, in persecutions, in distresses for Christ's sake: for <u>when I am weak, then am I strong.</u> 2 Corinthians 12:7-10

In his letter to the Ephesians, Paul, through the Holy Spirit, reveals some incredibly good news and gracious words of encouragement for anyone hungering and searching for truth, righteousness, and a victorious life of faith in Jesus.

For this cause I Paul, the prisoner of Jesus Christ <u>for you Gentiles</u>, If ye have heard of the dispensation of the grace of God which is given me to you-ward: How that by revelation he made known unto me the mystery; (as I wrote afore in few words, Whereby, when ye read, ye may understand my knowledge in the <u>mystery of Christ</u>) Which in other ages was not made known unto the sons of men, as it is now revealed

unto his holy apostles and prophets <u>by the Spirit</u>; <u>That the Gentiles should be fellowheirs, and of the same body, and partakers of his promise in Christ by the gospel</u>: Whereof I was made a minister, according to the gift of the grace of God given unto me by the effectual working of his power. Unto me, who am less than the least of all saints, is this grace given, that I should preach among the Gentiles <u>the unsearchable riches of Christ</u>; And to make all men see what is the fellowship of the mystery, which from the beginning of the world hath been hid in God, <u>who created all things by Jesus Christ</u>: To the intent that now unto the principalities and powers in heavenly places might be known <u>by the church</u> the manifold wisdom of God, According to the <u>eternal purpose</u> which he purposed in <u>Christ Jesus our Lord</u>: In whom we have boldness and access with confidence by the faith of him. Wherefore I desire that ye faint not at my tribulations for you, which is your glory. For this cause I bow my knees unto the Father of our Lord Jesus Christ, Of whom the whole family in heaven and earth is named, <u>That he would grant you, according to the riches of his glory, to be strengthened with might by his Spirit in the inner man; That Christ may dwell in your hearts by faith; that ye, being rooted and grounded in love, May be able to comprehend with all saints what is the breadth, and length, and depth, and height; And to know the love of Christ, which passeth knowledge, that ye might be filled with all the fulness of God.</u> Now unto him that is able to do exceeding abundantly above all that we ask or think, according to the power that worketh in us, Unto him be glory in the church by Christ Jesus throughout all ages, world without end. Amen. Ephesians 3

As we begin to comprehend our standing before God through our relationship with His Son Jesus, we will cease from striving for approval and simply rest in the arms of our Lord. We will learn to take His yoke upon us as we surrender our hearts and lives to Him each day. He will walk with us, never forsake us, and teach us what love really is and how much He loves us.

Beloved saints, let us draw near to our Lord each day and seek Him with all our hearts. In doing so, we will come to know the love of Christ and strength of might by His Spirit within us!

Come unto me, all ye that labour and are heavy laden, and <u>I will give you rest</u>. <u>Take my yoke upon you, and learn of me; for <u>I am meek and lowly in heart</u>: and <u>ye shall find rest unto your souls</u>. For my yoke is easy, and my burden is light. Matthew 11:28-30

The key for us is to abide in Him daily, as He very clearly taught us in John 15.

Andrew Murray, in his highly edifying book, "*Abide in Christ*", had this to say (underline my emphasis):

> "REST for the soul: Such was the first promise with which the Saviour sought to win the heavy-laden sinner. Simple though it appears, the promise is indeed as large and comprehensive as can be found. Rest for the soul - does it not imply deliverance from every fear, the supply of every want, the fulfilment of every desire? And now nothing less than this is the prize with which the Saviour woos back the wandering one - who is mourning that the rest has not been so abiding or so full as it had hoped - to come back and abide in Him. <u>Nothing but this was the reason that the rest has either not been found, or, if found, has been disturbed or lost again: you did not abide with, you did not abide in Him</u>.

Have you ever noticed how, in the original invitation of the Saviour to come to Him, the promise of rest was repeated twice, with such a variation in the conditions as might have suggested that abiding rest could only be found in abiding nearness. First the Saviour says, "Come unto me, and I will give you rest"; the very moment you come, and believe, I will give you rest - the rest of pardon and acceptance - the rest in my love. But we know that all that God bestows needs time to become fully our own; it must be held fast, and appropriated, and assimilated into our inmost being; without this not even Christ's giving can make it our very own, in full experience and enjoyment. And so the Saviour repeats His promise, in words which clearly speak not so much of the initial rest with which He welcomes the weary one who comes, but of the deeper and personally appropriated rest of the soul that abides with Him. He now not only says, "Come unto me," but "Take my yoke upon you and learn of me"; become my scholars, yield ourselves to my training, submit in all things to my will, let your whole life be one with mine - in other words, Abide in me. And then He adds, not only, "I will give," but "ye shall find rest to your souls." The rest He gave at coming will become something you have really found and made your very own- the deeper the abiding rest which comes from longer acquaintance and closer fellowship, from entire surrender and deeper sympathy. "Take my yoke, and learn of me," "Abide in me" - this is the path to abiding rest.

Do not these words of the Saviour discover what you have perhaps often sought in vain to know, how it is that the rest you at times enjoy is so often lost. It must have been this: you had not understood how entire surrender to Jesus is the secret of perfect rest. Giving up one's whole life to Him, for Him alone to rule and order it; taking up His yoke, and

118

submitting to be led and taught, to learn of Him; abiding in Him, to be and do only what He wills - these are the conditions of discipleship without which there can be no thought of maintaining the rest that was bestowed on first coming to Christ. The rest is in Christ, and not something He gives apart from Himself, and so it is only in having Him that the rest can really be kept and enjoyed.

It is because so many a young believer fails to lay hold of this truth that the rest so speedily passes away. With some it is that they really did not know; they were never taught how Jesus claims the undivided allegiance of the whole heart and life; how there is not a spot in the whole of life over which He does not wish to reign; how in the very least things His disciples must only seek to please Him. They did not know how entire the consecration was that Jesus claimed. With others, who had some idea of what a very holy life a Christian ought to lead, the mistake was a different one: they could not believe such a life to be a possible attainment. Taking, and bearing, and never for a moment laying aside the yoke of Jesus, appeared to them to require such a strain of effort, and such an amount of goodness, as to be altogether beyond their reach. The very idea of always, all the day, abiding in Jesus, was too high - something they might attain to after a life of holiness and growth, but certainly not what a feeble beginner was to start with. They did not know how, when Jesus said, "My yoke is easy," He spoke the truth; how just the yoke gives the rest, because the moment the soul yields itself to obey, the Lord Himself gives the strength and joy to do it. They did not notice how, when He said, "Learn of me," He added, "I am meek and lowly in heart," to assure them that His gentleness would meet their every need, and bear them as a mother bears her feeble child. Oh, they did not know that when He said, "Abide in me," He only asked the surrender to Himself, His almighty love would hold them fast, and keep and bless them. And so, as some had erred from the want of <u>full consecration,</u> so these failed because they did not <u>fully trust.</u> <u>These two, consecration and faith, are the essential elements of the Christian life-the giving up all to Jesus, the receiving all from Jesus. They are implied in each other; they are united in the one word-surrender. A full surrender is to obey as well as to trust, to trust as well as to obey.</u>

With such misunderstanding at the outset, it is no wonder that the disciple life was not one of such joy or strength as had been hoped. In some things you were led into sin without knowing it, because you had not learned how wholly Jesus wanted to rule you, and how you could not keep right for a moment unless you had Him very near you. In other things you knew what sin was, but had not the power to conquer, because you did not know or believe how entirely Jesus would take charge of you to keep and to help you. Either way, it was not long before the bright joy of your first love was lost, and your path, instead of being like the path of the just, shining more and more unto the perfect day, became like Israel's wandering in the desert ever on the way, never very far, and yet always coming short of the promised rest. Weary soul, since so many years driven to and fro like the panting hart, O come and learn this day the lesson that there is a spot where safety and victory, where peace and rest, are always sure, and that that spot is always open to thee-the heart of Jesus.

But, alas! I hear someone say, it is just this abiding in Jesus, always bearing His yoke, to learn of Him, that is so difficult, and the very effort to attain to this often disturbs the rest even more than sin or the world. What a mistake to speak thus, and yet how often the words are heard! Does it weary the traveller to rest in the house or on the bed where he seeks repose from his fatigue? Or is it a labour to a little child to rest in its mother's arms? Is it not the house that keeps the traveller within its shelter? Do not the arms of the mother sustain and keep the little one? And so it is with Jesus. The soul has but to yield itself to Him, to be still and rest in the confidence that His love has undertaken, and that His faithfulness will perform, the work of keeping it safe in the shelter of His bosom. Oh, it is because the blessing is so great that our little hearts cannot rise to apprehend it; it is as if we cannot believe that Christ, the Almighty One, will in very deed teach and keep us all the day. And yet this is just what He has promised, for without this He cannot really give us rest. It is as our heart takes in this truth that, when He says, "Abide in me," "Learn of me," He really means it, and that it is His own work to keep us abiding when we yield ourselves to Him, that we shall venture to cast ourselves into the arms of His love, and abandon ourselves to His blessed keeping. It is not the yoke, but resistance to the yoke, that makes the difficulty; the wholehearted surrender to Jesus, as at once our Master and our Keeper, finds and secures the rest.

Come, my brother, and let us this very day commence to accept the word of Jesus in all simplicity. It is a distinct command this: "Take my yoke, and learn of me," "Abide in me." A command has to be obeyed. The obedient scholar asks no questions about possibilities or results; he accepts every order in the confidence that his teacher has provided for all that is needed. The power and the perseverance to abide in the rest, and the blessing in abiding - it belongs to the Saviour to see to this; 'tis mine to obey, 'tis His to provide. Let us this day in immediate obedience accept the command, and answer boldly, "Saviour, I abide in Thee. At Thy bidding I take Thy yoke; I undertake the duty without delay; I abide in Thee." Let each consciousness of failure only give new urgency to the command, and teach us to listen more earnestly than ever till the Spirit again give us to hear the voice of Jesus saying, with a love and authority that inspire both hope and obedience, "Child, abide in me." That word, listened to as coming from Himself, will be an end of all doubting-a divine promise of what shall surely be granted. And with ever-increasing simplicity its meaning will be interpreted. Abiding in Jesus is nothing but the giving up of oneself to be ruled and taught and led, and so resting in the arms of Everlasting Love.

Blessed rest! The fruit and the foretaste and the fellowship of God's own rest! Found of them who thus come to Jesus to abide in Him. It is the peace of God, the great calm of the eternal world, that passeth all understanding, and that keeps the heart and mind. With this grace secured, we have strength for every duty, courage for every struggle, a blessing in every cross, and the joy of life eternal in death itself.

O my Saviour! If ever my heart should doubt or fear again, as if the blessing were too great to expect, or too high to attain, let me hear Thy voice to quicken my faith and obedience: "Abide in me"; "Take my yoke upon you, and learn of me; ye shall find rest to your souls." - Andrew Murray, *Abide in Christ*

Dear reader, once we understand the importance of abiding in Jesus and make that our goal every day, then we will be able to overcome sin, the world, our flesh and Satan. We will have found the secret to the power of Christ in us and rest for our souls.

Ye are of God, little children, and have overcome them: because <u>greater is he that is in you</u>, than he that is in the world. 1 John 4:4

We receive the priceless gift of the Power of Christ in our fragile flesh for a very specific purpose. It is precisely so that we do NOT exalt ourselves in the vanity of our minds and selfish pride, which is the same deceptive sin that caused Lucifer (Satan) to fall and defeated Adam and Eve as well. Read carefully the following words of the apostle Paul in his letter to the Corinthians:

Therefore seeing we have this ministry, as <u>we have received mercy</u>, we faint not; But <u>have renounced the hidden things of dishonesty</u>, not walking in craftiness, nor handling the word of God deceitfully; but by manifestation of the truth commending ourselves to every man's conscience in the sight of God. But if our gospel be hid, <u>it is hid to them that are lost</u>: In whom the god of this world (Satan) <u>hath blinded the minds of them which believe not</u>, lest the light of the glorious <u>gospel of Christ</u>, who is the image of God, should shine unto them. For we preach not ourselves, but Christ Jesus the Lord; and ourselves your servants for Jesus' sake. For God, who commanded the light to shine out of darkness, <u>hath shined in our hearts</u>, to give the light of the knowledge of the glory of God in the face of Jesus Christ. <u>But we have this treasure in earthen vessels, that the excellency of the power may be of God, and not of us</u>. 2 Corinthians 4:1-7

God, in His unsearchable wisdom, grants us His power in our hearts through our relationship with His beloved Son and does so to teach us to get out of our own way and let His love work through us to others.

Therefore being justified by faith, we have peace with God through our Lord Jesus Christ: By whom also we have access by faith into this grace wherein we stand, and rejoice in hope of the glory of God. And not only so, but we glory in tribulations also: knowing that tribulation worketh patience; And patience, experience; and experience, hope: And hope maketh not ashamed; <u>because the love of God is shed abroad in our hearts by the Holy Ghost which is given unto us</u>. Romans 5:1-5

Now we can begin to understand exactly what the Power of Christ in us is. <u>It is nothing less than the power to love</u>! When we long to know Jesus more and more, we will seek to draw closer to Him and our love for Him will grow ever more powerful and deep day by day. He will manifest His love for us in us and through us to those around us.

If you are a believer, you will love Jesus as your first love. You will come to disallow anything or anyone to come between you and the Lord. Your love for Jesus will grow as you grow in your understanding of just how much He loves you and what it cost Him to prove it. The words He spoke to Simon, the Pharisee, certainly speak to my own heart.

And one of the Pharisees desired him that he would eat with him. And he went into the Pharisee's house, and sat down to meat. And, behold, a woman in the city, which was a sinner, when she knew that Jesus sat at meat in the Pharisee's house, brought an alabaster box of ointment, And stood at his feet behind him weeping, and began to wash his feet with tears, and did wipe them with the hairs of her head, and kissed his feet,

and anointed them with the ointment. Now when the Pharisee which had bidden him saw it, he spake within himself, saying, This man, if he were a prophet, would have known who and what manner of woman this is that toucheth him: for she is a sinner. And Jesus answering said unto him, Simon, I have somewhat to say unto thee. And he saith, Master, say on. There was a certain creditor which had two debtors: the one owed five hundred pence, and the other fifty. And when they had nothing to pay, he frankly forgave them both. Tell me therefore, which of them will love him most? Simon answered and said, I suppose that he, to whom he forgave most. And he said unto him, Thou hast rightly judged. And he turned to the woman, and said unto Simon, Seest thou this woman? I entered into thine house, thou gavest me no water for my feet: but she hath washed my feet with tears, and wiped them with the hairs of her head. Thou gavest me no kiss: but this woman since the time I came in hath not ceased to kiss my feet. My head with oil thou didst not anoint: but this woman hath anointed my feet with ointment. <u>Wherefore I say unto thee, Her sins, which are many, are forgiven; for she loved much: but to whom little is forgiven, the same loveth little</u>. And he said unto her, Thy sins are forgiven. And they that sat at meat with him began to say within themselves, Who is this that forgiveth sins also? And he said to the woman, Thy faith hath saved thee; go in peace. Luke 7:36-50

I am so thankful that the sins of this wretched man (me) have been forgiven by the One I love with all my heart. Thank You Jesus, for saving me and teaching me what is right in Thy Father's sight. Thank You for the many tender mercies and loving kindnesses that You have so patiently blessed me with; even when I walked in the selfishness of my wretched vanity.

Over the last few years, in my own walk with Jesus, my heart has longed to know Him more intimately and fully. The words of John the Baptist started echoing in my ears as I realized that I must become less and He must become more. I began to see things in a new perspective where, when confronted with temptations and trials that I was facing each day, my first thought became, "I love Jesus more". In other words, I began to choose to love Jesus more than whatever yielding to the temptations of the hour might do for me. It has become more and more important to me that I take care of my Master's heart as best as I can, and I can do that when it concerns my actions. I do not want to grieve His heart or the precious Holy Spirit He has so graciously put in mine.

Through studying the way He lived His life on this earth, the things He taught, the amazing and miraculous good deeds He did for so many, the numerous prophetic Scriptures that were directly and completely fulfilled by Him in His birth, life, death, and resurrection, the way He changed EVERYONE who He came into contact with (who either repented or rebelled), my relationship with Jesus has been deeply affected. I have come to love Him more and more and more for what He did for me and will do for anyone who comes to Him and remains in Him.

As a believer, have you ever wondered what you might do or say when you finally get the opportunity to meet Jesus and your faith becomes sight? Have you thought you might fall down at His feet, run up and hug Him, weep tears of joy or sing songs of praise and victory, dance for Him in sheer joy, or perhaps not be able to speak at all? What would you do if you know Jesus and met Him tonight, or tomorrow morning? I have thought about that, as I am sure most believers have.

Recently, the thought occurred to me that when I finally get to see Jesus face to face, what if before I will be able to do or say anything, He makes me sit down and then proceeds to wash MY feet? How would you respond to such an act? Is THE Son of God humbling Himself before me and washing my feet? "Stunned" would be an understatement I am sure! You see, when Jesus humbled himself and washed the apostle's feet at the last supper, He was revealing to them His heart on a most personal level. I am sure that they were speechless as well. That is, except for my brother Peter, who I completely empathize with!

What was Jesus teaching His followers? The most important lesson of all – the power of Christ is the power of love and the power to love!

Who shall separate us from <u>the love of Christ</u>? shall tribulation, or distress, or persecution, or famine, or nakedness, or peril, or sword? As it is written, For thy sake we are killed all the day long; we are accounted as sheep for the slaughter. Nay, <u>in all these things we are more than conquerors through him that loved us</u>. For I am persuaded, that neither death, nor life, nor angels, nor principalities, nor powers, nor things present, nor things to come, Nor height, nor depth, nor any other creature, shall be able to separate us from the love of God, <u>which is in Christ Jesus our Lord</u>. Romans 8:35-39

For all the law is fulfilled in one word, even in this; Thou shalt <u>love</u> thy neighbour as thyself. Galatians 5:14

Once again, Jesus tells us what is the most important thing for us to know and live by:

I am the true vine, and my Father is the husbandman. Every branch in me that beareth not fruit he taketh away: and every branch that beareth fruit, he purgeth it, that it may bring forth more fruit. Now ye are clean through the word which I have

spoken unto you. Abide in me, and I in you. As the branch cannot bear fruit of itself, except it abide in the vine; no more can ye, except ye abide in me. I am the vine, ye are the branches: He that abideth in me, and I in him, the same bringeth forth much fruit: <u>for without me ye can do nothing</u>. If a man abide not in me, he is cast forth as a branch, and is withered; and men gather them, and cast them into the fire, and they are burned. If ye abide in me, and my words abide in you, ye shall ask what ye will, and it shall be done unto you. Herein is my Father glorified, that ye bear much fruit; so shall ye be my disciples. As the Father hath loved me, so have I loved you: <u>continue ye in my love. If ye keep my commandments, ye shall abide in my love; even as I have kept my Father's commandments, and abide in his love</u>. These things have I spoken unto you, that my joy might remain in you, and that your joy might be full. <u>This is my commandment, That ye love one another, as I have loved you. Greater love hath no man than this, that a man lay down his life for his friends. Ye are my friends, if ye do whatsoever I command you</u>. Henceforth I call you not servants; for the servant knoweth not what his lord doeth: but I have called you friends; for all things that I have heard of my Father I have made known unto you. Ye have not chosen me, but I have chosen you, and ordained you, that ye should go and bring forth fruit, and that your fruit should remain: that whatsoever ye shall ask of the Father in my name, he may give it you. <u>These things I command you, that ye love one another</u>. John 15

Love is everything. Love conquers all. Love is a fulfillment of all the law and the prophets. Love seeks another's best interests over one's own. Love keeps no record of wrongs, is kind, is patient, does not envy, is not proud, does not behave unseemly, is not easily provoked, seeks no evil, does not rejoice in iniquity but rejoices in the truth. Love bears all things, believes all things, hopes all things, and endures all things. Love never fails (1 Corinthians 13)

This is the power of Christ in you.

Jesus tells us how we can be blessed, as well as the attitudes in our hearts and actions in our lives that should be evident for that to occur.

And seeing the multitudes, he went up into a mountain: and when he was set, his disciples came unto him: And he opened his mouth, and taught them, saying,

Blessed are the poor in spirit: for theirs is the kingdom of heaven.

Why? Because only the poor in spirit will have come to the end of themselves and have hearts that are open to receive the truth.

Blessed are they that mourn: for they shall be comforted.

Why? The poor in spirit are mourning the failure in their lives as a result of their own efforts.

Blessed are the meek: for they shall inherit the earth.

Why? Those who are ashamed acknowledge their failure in sin and are humble, not proud.

Blessed are they which do hunger and thirst after righteousness: for they shall be filled.

Why? The poor in spirit, the meek, and the humble know that they are lacking what they really long for and this is the beginning of the narrow road.

Blessed are the merciful: for they shall obtain mercy.

Why? Those who have been granted mercy and forgiveness will have a heart that grants mercy unto others.

Blessed are the pure in heart: for they shall see God.

Why? Those who have obtained mercy have been born again with a new heart that is filled with the Holy Spirit as they obey the Spirit of Truth.

Blessed are the peacemakers: for they shall be called the children of God.

Why? The pure in heart obey the Prince of Peace and love others as themselves.

Blessed are they which are persecuted for righteousness' sake: for theirs is the kingdom of heaven.

Why? Friendship with the world is enmity with God. What the world values is abominable to God.

Blessed are ye, when men shall revile you, and persecute you, and shall say all manner of evil against you falsely, for my sake.

Why? Darkness hates the light because it exposes the evil deeds of the workers of iniquity and testifies to their guilt.

Rejoice, and be exceeding glad: for great is your reward in heaven: for so persecuted they the prophets which were before you.

Ye are the salt of the earth: but if the salt have lost his savour, wherewith shall it be salted? <u>it is thenceforth good for nothing, but to be cast out, and to be trodden under foot of men.</u>

Saving faith is like salt that prevents rot and decay in a corrupt world.

Ye are the light of the world. <u>A city that is set on an hill cannot be hid.</u>

Neither do men light a candle, and put it under a bushel, but on a candlestick; <u>and it giveth light unto all that are in the house.</u>

Saving faith is like a light that shines in the darkness to reprove evil and testify to the truth.

Let your light so shine before men, that they may see your good works, and glorify your Father which is in heaven. Matthew 5:1-16

In summary, we know that our faith in Jesus requires obedience and we know that, in our own power, we do not have the ability to by holy. So, we must trust in the power of Christ in us and yield our hearts to Him in order to overcome and be pleasing to the Father. The apostle Peter tells us how to do just that:

Simon Peter, a servant and an apostle of Jesus Christ, to them that have obtained like precious faith with us through the righteousness of God and our Saviour Jesus Christ: Grace and peace be multiplied unto you through the knowledge of God, and of Jesus our Lord, According as <u>his divine power hath given unto us all things that pertain unto life and godliness,</u> through the knowledge of him that hath called us to glory and

virtue: Whereby are given unto us exceeding great and precious promises: that by these ye might be partakers of the divine nature, having escaped the corruption that is in the world through lust. 2 Peter 1:1-4

As my brother and pastor of a church in Ohio recently stated:

"In America, there are many professors of faith. Let us be possessors of faith." Greg DiMeolo

I would like to close this chapter with some words of wisdom that the Holy Spirit spoke through Paul in his letter to the Philippians. As believers, in order for us to overcome and live holy and pleasing to God, one of the things we must do is walk with renewed minds while we wear the helmet of salvation; along with all the other armor of God. Paul tells us how to do that:

Rejoice in the Lord always: and again I say, Rejoice. Let your moderation be known unto all men. The Lord is at hand. Be careful for nothing; but in every thing by <u>prayer</u> and <u>supplication</u> with <u>thanksgiving</u> let your requests be made known unto God. And <u>the peace of God</u>, which passeth all understanding, <u>shall keep your hearts and minds through Christ Jesus.</u> Finally, brethren, whatsoever things are <u>true</u>, whatsoever things are <u>honest</u>, whatsoever things are <u>just</u>, whatsoever things are <u>pure</u>, whatsoever things are <u>lovely</u>, whatsoever things are of <u>good report</u>; if there be any <u>virtue</u>, and if there be any <u>praise</u>, <u>think on these things</u>. Philippians 4:4-8

Heavenly Father, thank You for loving me so much that You sent Jesus to save me. Thank You for the precious gift of the Holy Spirit, which is the power of Christ in me to love unconditionally and freely. Thank You, Holy Spirit for being my Comforter and for

guiding me daily into all truth. Please continue to be a lamp unto my feet and a light unto my path so that I remain in Christ Jesus on the narrow road that leads to eternal life and bear much good fruit for Your Kingdom. In the name of Jesus I pray, Amen.

Chapter 7

SAUL THE PHARISEE VERSUS PAUL THE APOSTLE

And he said, Who art thou, Lord? And the Lord said, I am Jesus whom thou persecutest: it is hard for thee to kick against the pricks. Acts 9:5

The man, who through inspiration of the Holy Spirit wrote much of the New Testament, is someone we certainly want to know about. Just who was Saul (also called Paul), and how did he fit into God's plan for the redemption of mankind and the revelation of The Redeemer, Jesus? Understanding the story of Paul will greatly strengthen our faith in, and love for, our Savior as we learn about God's manifold wisdom and unsearchable love He has for us.

Our initial experience with Saul is certainly not an impressive one. As a matter of fact, when we first read about him in the book of Acts, I venture to say that most of us would find him a highly repugnant, black-hearted, arrogant, self-righteous know-it-all! Likewise, I cannot imagine any of us thinking that this person would be the ideal individual to proclaim the truth of Jesus Christ to the world. As we pick up the story, we see that Saul is present and consenting to the murder of Stephen; a faithful believer on the Lord Jesus who spoke the truth to the hypocritical religious leaders of Israel. Stephen spoke the truth when he said:

Ye stiffnecked and uncircumcised in heart and ears, <u>ye do always resist the Holy Ghost</u>: as your fathers did, so do ye. Which of the prophets have not your fathers persecuted? and they <u>have slain them which shewed before of the coming of the Just One</u>; of whom ye <u>have been now the betrayers and murderers</u>: Who have received the law by the disposition of angels, <u>and have not kept it</u>. When they heard these things, <u>they were cut to the heart</u>, and they gnashed on him with their teeth. But he, <u>being full of the Holy Ghost</u>, looked up stedfastly into heaven, and saw the glory of God, and <u>Jesus</u> standing on the right hand of God, And said, Behold, I see the heavens opened, and <u>the Son of man</u> standing on the right hand of God. Then they cried out with a loud voice, and stopped their ears, and ran upon him with one accord, <u>And cast him out of the city</u>, <u>and stoned him</u>: and the witnesses laid down their clothes at a young man's feet, <u>whose name was Saul. And they stoned Stephen</u>, calling upon God, and saying, <u>Lord Jesus</u>, receive my spirit. Acts 7:51-59

So, we learn that Saul had no problem judging others with a cold, calculating harshness that had no limits, no love, and absolutely no mercy. The death of the innocent man Stephen does not bother Saul in the least! How do we know this? Unfortunately, Saul's subsequent actions speak for themselves and give us much insight as to exactly who this man is.

And <u>Saul was consenting unto his death</u>. And at that time there was a great persecution against the church which was at Jerusalem; and they were all scattered abroad throughout the regions of Judaea and Samaria, except the apostles. And devout men carried Stephen to his burial, and made great lamentation over him. <u>As for Saul, he made havock of the church, entering into every house, and haling men and women committed them to prison</u>. Acts 8:1-3

His zeal for the law and traditions of his religion had blinded Saul to the truth that Jesus so earnestly tried to remind his fellow Pharisees and Sadducees of. Who was it that Jesus was most angry with? Who was it that Jesus rebuked in the strongest terms possible? Who was it that Jesus called out as the most opposed to the truth, the most dangerous to the souls of men, and the most obstinately resistant to the Kingdom of God? I tremble when I read the words that the Son of God spoke to the religious leaders of Israel, because Jesus is the One to whom the Father has given ALL authority to judge mankind. Jesus said:

But <u>woe unto you, scribes and Pharisees, hypocrites</u>! for ye shut up the kingdom of heaven against men: for ye neither go in yourselves, neither suffer ye them that are entering to go in. <u>Woe unto you, scribes and Pharisees, hypocrites</u>! for ye devour widows' houses, and for a pretence make long prayer: therefore ye shall receive the greater damnation. <u>Woe unto you, scribes and Pharisees, hypocrites</u>! for ye compass sea and land to make one proselyte, and when he is made, ye make him twofold more the child of hell than yourselves. <u>Woe unto you, ye blind guides</u>, which say, Whosoever shall swear by the temple, it is nothing; but whosoever shall swear by the gold of the temple, he is a debtor! Ye <u>fools</u> and <u>blind</u>: for whether is greater, the gold, or the temple that sanctifieth the gold? And, Whosoever shall swear by the altar, it is nothing; but whosoever sweareth by the gift that is upon it, he is guilty. Ye <u>fools</u> and <u>blind</u>: for whether is greater, the gift, or the altar that sanctifieth the gift? Whoso therefore shall swear by the altar, sweareth by it, and by all things thereon. And whoso shall swear by the temple, sweareth by it, and by him that dwelleth therein. And he that shall swear by heaven, sweareth by the throne of God, and by him that sitteth thereon. <u>Woe unto you, scribes and Pharisees, hypocrites</u>! for ye pay tithe of mint and anise and cummin, and have omitted the weightier

matters of the law, judgment, mercy, and faith: these ought ye to have done, and not to leave the other undone. Ye <u>blind guides</u>, which strain at a gnat, and swallow a camel. <u>Woe unto you, scribes and Pharisees, hypocrites</u>! for ye make clean the outside of the cup and of the platter, but within they are full of extortion and excess. Thou <u>blind Pharisee</u>, cleanse first that which is within the cup and platter, that the outside of them may be clean also. <u>Woe unto you, scribes and Pharisees, hypocrites</u>! for ye are like unto whited sepulchres, which indeed appear beautiful outward, but are within <u>full of dead men's bones</u>, and of <u>all uncleanness</u>. Even so ye also outwardly appear righteous unto men, but within <u>ye are full of hypocrisy and iniquity</u>. Woe unto you, scribes and Pharisees, hypocrites! because ye build the tombs of the prophets, and garnish the sepulchres of the righteous, And say, If we had been in the days of our fathers, we would not have been partakers with them in the blood of the prophets. Wherefore ye be witnesses unto yourselves, that <u>ye are the children of them which killed the prophets</u>. Fill ye up then the measure of your fathers. <u>Ye serpents, ye generation of vipers, how can ye escape the damnation of hell</u>? Wherefore, behold, I send unto you prophets, and wise men, and scribes: and some of them ye shall kill and crucify; and some of them shall ye scourge in your synagogues, and persecute them from city to city: <u>That upon you may come all the righteous blood shed upon the earth, from the blood of righteous Abel unto the blood of Zacharias son of Barachias, whom ye slew between the temple and the altar</u>. Verily I say unto you, All these things shall come upon this generation. O Jerusalem, Jerusalem, thou that <u>killest the prophets</u>, and <u>stonest them which are sent unto thee</u>, how often would I have gathered thy children together, even as a hen gathereth her chickens under her wings, and ye would not! <u>Behold, your house is left unto you desolate</u>. For I say unto

137

you, Ye shall not see me henceforth, till ye shall say, Blessed is he that cometh in the name of the Lord. Matthew 23:13-39

This is the heart of Saul; the heart of a religious zealot who is not concerned with justice, mercy or truth, but rather self-aggrandizement (the act or practice of enhancing or exaggerating one's own importance, power, or reputation); self-justification; and self-righteousness among the people. Saul's passion was the justification of his religion at all costs; a pattern that has, tragically, been repeated many times over the course of history and is commonly seen today as well in those religions that manifest the fruit of hatred and teach their adherents to live by the sword. To think that one can force their system of beliefs on others under threat of violence is nothing less than outright hatred, the manifestation of pure evil, and an absolute abomination in the eyes of God.

Jesus warned His followers:

These things have I spoken unto you, that ye should not be offended. They shall put you out of the synagogues: yea, <u>the time cometh, that whosoever killeth you will think that he doeth God service</u>. And these things will they do unto you, because they have not known the Father, nor me. John 16:1-3

Returning to the story of Saul, it was not enough for him to persecute the followers of Jesus in Jerusalem; he was a man on a mission to wipe out all vestiges of Christian faith in the region and received authority from the religious leaders to do so. However, what happened next was not on Saul's check list of "To do" items:

And <u>Saul</u>, yet breathing out threatenings and slaughter against the disciples of the Lord, went unto the high priest, And desired of him letters to Damascus to the synagogues, that if he

138

found any of this way, whether they were men or women, he might bring them bound unto Jerusalem. And as he journeyed, he came near Damascus: and suddenly there shined round about him a light from heaven: And he fell to the earth, and heard a voice saying unto him, Saul, Saul, why persecutest thou me? And he said, Who art thou, Lord? And the Lord said, <u>I am Jesus whom thou persecutest</u>: it is hard for thee to kick against the pricks. Acts 9:1-5

Now, I must ask, have you ever given all of your heart, mind and effort in passionate pursuit of an ideal that you thoroughly believed in, only to suddenly find out that you were wrong? If so, you can imagine how Saul must have felt at that moment; only in his case, there was innocent blood on his hands and he now knew it! He was face-to-face with the risen Savior who was confronting him with that horrible reality! In this moment of awakening, he even acknowledges the One, whose followers he was persecuting, as Lord! How would you have responded to such a revelation? How would anyone? Saul instantly realized that his life he had been living was grossly in error and was actually leading him to death and destruction. He responded to Jesus:

And he trembling and astonished said, Lord, what wilt thou have me to do? And the Lord said unto him, Arise, and go into the city, and it shall be told thee what thou must do. And the men which journeyed with him stood speechless, hearing a voice, but seeing no man. And Saul arose from the earth; and when his eyes were opened, he saw no man: but they led him by the hand, and brought him into Damascus. <u>And he was three days without sight, and neither did eat nor drink</u>. Acts 9:6-9

I submit to you, dear reader, that those three days Saul spent in the dark were the longest of his life! The teachings and traditions that he had held so close to his heart and followed so passionately in his life had somehow become a perverse mutation of the pure doctrine given to his forefathers by God himself! How had he so miscalculated, misinterpreted, misrepresented and miss-applied what was supposed to by holy and true and pure? I am certain that Saul spent many hours agonizing over this; praying long and hard about what would happen to him next. It is very likely that Saul was thinking that he might be under the final judgment of God and that he would never see again and probably be eternally condemned; a terrifying prospect for the once Pharisee of Pharisees. The truth, however, was beyond Saul's comprehension! Beloved saints and those who want to know Jesus, let us give thanks and praise that our Heavenly Father and His beloved Son are full of tender mercies and loving kindnesses!

And there was a certain disciple at Damascus, named Ananias; and to him said the Lord in a vision, Ananias. And he said, Behold, I am here, Lord. And the Lord said unto him, Arise, and go into the street which is called Straight, and enquire in the house of Judas for one called <u>Saul, of Tarsus</u>: for, behold, <u>he prayeth</u>, And hath seen in a vision a man named Ananias coming in, and putting his hand on him, that he might receive his sight. Then Ananias answered, Lord, I have heard by many of this man, <u>how much evil he hath done to thy saints</u> at Jerusalem: And here he hath authority from the chief priests to bind all that call on thy name. But the Lord said unto him, Go thy way: <u>for he is a chosen vessel unto me, to bear my name before the Gentiles, and kings, and the children of Israel: For I will shew him how great things he must suffer for my name's sake.</u> Acts 9:10-16

Wow! Read that last part again! Jesus just told Ananias that Saul, the lead persecutor of the believers of the Lord, the one responsible for their imprisonment, <u>will be the very one to bear His name</u>

before the gentiles, kings, and the very people of Israel! Saul has been commissioned by Jesus to be His witness to The Truth - Jesus is the Messiah, the Savior, and the way of salvation for everyone! When we look at this event from a historical perspective, we can now see the perfect wisdom of our Lord Jesus in selecting this man to be the apostle to the world. Saul now becomes a born again believer and follower of Jesus and proceeds to take the world by storm!

And Ananias went his way, and entered into the house; and putting his hands on him said, Brother Saul, <u>the Lord, even Jesus</u>, that appeared unto thee in the way as thou camest, hath sent me, that thou mightest receive thy sight, and <u>be filled with the Holy Ghost</u>. And immediately there fell from his eyes as it had been scales: and he received sight forthwith, and arose, and was baptized. And when he had received meat, he was strengthened. Then was Saul certain days with the disciples which were at Damascus. And straightway he preached Christ in the synagogues, that <u>he is the Son of God</u>. But all that heard him were amazed, and said; Is not this he that destroyed them <u>which called on this name</u> in Jerusalem, and came hither for that intent, that he might bring them bound unto the chief priests? But Saul increased the more in strength, and confounded the Jews which dwelt at Damascus, <u>proving that this is very Christ</u>. Acts 9:17-22

Who better to be a powerful witness to the truth than a man well known for passionately opposing it? To say that something of great significance happened that caused an abrupt change in this Pharisee's heart would be an understatement! Amazingly, now that Saul's eyes have been opened to the truth, guess what his Pharisee "Brothers" decide they must do?

And after that many days were fulfilled, the Jews took counsel to <u>kill him</u>: But their laying await was known of Saul. And they watched the gates day and night to <u>kill him</u>. Acts 9:23, 24

Their plans for the destruction of Saul where spoiled however, as the disciples rescued him, and the beloved brother Barnabus assisted him greatly by vouching for Saul and the genuineness of his conversion. As a result, he was now able to associate with the very disciples in Jerusalem that he had previously been persecuting! Soon, however, others who Saul disputed with sought to kill him as well, so the disciples sent Saul to Tarsus.

Then the disciples took him by night, and let him down by the wall in a basket. And when Saul was come to Jerusalem, he assayed to join himself to the disciples: but they were all afraid of him, and believed not that he was a disciple. But <u>Barnabas</u> took him, and brought him to the apostles, and declared unto them how he had seen the Lord in the way, and that he had spoken to him, and how he had preached boldly at Damascus in the name of Jesus. And he was with them coming in and going out at Jerusalem. And he spake boldly in the name of the Lord Jesus, and disputed against the Grecians: <u>but they went about to slay him</u>. Which when the brethren knew, they brought him down to Caesarea, and sent him forth to Tarsus. Then had the churches rest throughout all Judaea and Galilee and Samaria, and were edified; and <u>walking in the fear of the Lord</u>, and <u>in the comfort of the Holy Ghost</u>, were multiplied. Acts 9:25-31

After meeting Jesus, what changed in Paul's heart and what became his driving passion? The revelation of the truth of exactly who Jesus is changed the man for the rest of his life and obeying the Lord became his passion above all else! As a believer, Paul now realized that all his training, education, rituals, and accomplishments as a zealous Pharisee meant nothing to him when compared to <u>knowing Jesus!</u> What an amazing and nothing short of miraculous re-birth for this man! The apostle leaves no room for doubt as he tells us clearly in his own words:

Finally, my brethren, <u>rejoice in the Lord</u>. To write the same things to you, to me indeed is not grievous, but for you it is safe. Beware of dogs, beware of evil workers, beware of the concision. For we are the circumcision, which <u>worship God in the spirit</u>, and <u>rejoice in Christ Jesus</u>, and <u>have no confidence in the flesh</u>. Though I might also have confidence in the flesh. If any other man thinketh that he hath whereof he might trust in the flesh, I more: Circumcised the eighth day, of the stock of Israel, of the tribe of Benjamin, an Hebrew of the Hebrews; as touching the law, a Pharisee; Concerning zeal, persecuting the church; touching the righteousness which is in the law, blameless. <u>But what things were gain to me, those I counted loss for Christ</u>. <u>Yea doubtless, and I count all things but loss for the excellency of the knowledge of Christ Jesus my Lord: for whom I have suffered the loss of all things, and do count them but dung, that I may win Christ,</u>

Paul is saying that without a relationship with Jesus, nothing matters; nothing has value; all other effort is in fact useless to our souls and repulsive to God!

<u>And be found in him, not having mine own righteousness, which is of the law, but that which is through the faith of Christ, the righteousness which is of God by faith</u>:

This is the TRUE Gospel. Without a relationship with Jesus by faith, there is NO righteousness for any man!

143

That I may know him, and the power of his resurrection, and the fellowship of his sufferings, being made conformable unto his death;

Knowing Jesus is EVERYTHING! Not knowing Him is the loss of everything that matters.

If by any means I might attain unto the resurrection of the dead. Not as though I had already attained, either were already perfect: but I follow after, if that I may apprehend that for which also I am apprehended of Christ Jesus.

WARNING: If you are comfortable with your belief in the OSAS – Once Saved Always Saved doctrine, then read the words of Paul above. This faithful apostle to the world did not consider himself to have already obtained salvation. He knew that the promise of eternal life was conditional and required obedience on his part.

Brethren, I count not myself to have apprehended: but this one thing I do, forgetting those things which are behind, and reaching forth unto those things which are before, I press toward the mark for the prize of the high calling of God in Christ Jesus. Philippians 3:1-14

Dear reader, this is a very comforting Scripture for all of us who are hungering and searching for righteousness. Why? Because, like Paul, we know that we have stumbled in the past and sinned against God.

If we confess our sins, he is faithful and just to forgive us our sins, and to cleanse us from all unrighteousness. 1 John 1:9

What that means to us is that we stop habitually sinning for, without holiness, no one shall see the Lord.

Follow peace with all men, and holiness, without which no man shall see the Lord: Hebrews 12:14

How did Paul spend the rest of his life after encountering the Son of the Living God, the Messiah Jesus?

He travelled on three missionary journeys throughout the ancient world, witnessing to the truth of Jesus Christ as the Messiah of the Jews and Savior of the Gentiles.

He wrote most of the New Testament and established the Christian faith among the nations, resulting in approximately one out of three today who call themselves Christian.

He was second only to Jesus in proclaiming the truth of the Gospel.

He established at least fourteen and most likely twenty plus Christian churches.

He was whipped <u>five</u> times with 39 lashes, beaten with rods, and hit with stones until presumed dead.

He was ship wrecked three times and spent a night and day in the sea.

He was in constant danger of being murdered by his own countrymen and was specifically rescued by the Roman army on one occasion when 40 of them took an oath to kill him (see Acts 23:12-35).

He was falsely accused, falsely imprisoned, and taken as a prisoner to Rome where he was murdered for the cause of Jesus Christ.

"Paul, the apostle, who before was called Saul, after his great travail and unspeakable labors in promoting the Gospel of Christ, suffered also in this first persecution under Nero. Abdias, declareth that under his execution Nero sent two of his esquires, Ferega and Parthemius, to bring him word of his death. They, coming to Paul instructing the people, desired him to pray for them, that they might believe; who told them that shortly after they should believe and be baptised at His sepulcher. This done, the soldiers came and led him out of the city to the place of execution, where he, after his prayers made, gave his neck to the sword." *Foxe's Book of Martyrs*

Is there any question in anyone's mind that the Pharisee turned apostle Paul did one simple thing and did it extraordinarily well?

He heard the voice of Jesus and obeyed.

He is set forth as an example for all of us to draw ever closer to our first love and obey Him, no matter the cost. Jesus indeed showed Paul how much the latter must suffer for the Lord's name. Through the Holy Spirit, Paul has given us much truth that we can apply in our walk with Jesus as Christians in a corrupt world. In closing his letter to the church at Ephesus, Paul wrote:

Children, <u>obey your parents in the Lord</u>: for this is right. Honour thy father and mother; which is the first commandment with promise; <u>That it may be well with thee</u>, and <u>thou mayest live long on the earth</u>. And, ye fathers, provoke not your children to wrath: but <u>bring them up in the nurture and admonition of the Lord</u>. Servants, be obedient to them that are your masters according to the flesh, with fear and trembling, in singleness of your heart, as unto Christ; Not with eyeservice, as menpleasers; but as the servants of Christ, doing the will of God from the heart; With good will doing service, as to the Lord, and not to men: Knowing that

whatsoever good thing any man doeth, the same shall he receive of the Lord, whether he be bond or free. And, ye masters, do the same things unto them, forbearing threatening: knowing that your Master also is in heaven; neither is there respect of persons with him. Finally, my brethren, <u>be strong in the Lord, and in the power of his might.</u> <u>Put on the whole armour of God</u>, that ye may be able to stand against the wiles of the devil. <u>For we wrestle not against flesh and blood, but against principalities, against powers, against the rulers of the darkness of this world, against spiritual wickedness in high places.</u> Wherefore take unto you the whole armour of God, that ye may be able to withstand in the evil day, and having done all, <u>to stand.</u> Stand therefore, <u>having your loins girt about with truth</u>, and <u>having on the breastplate of righteousness;</u> And <u>your feet shod with the preparation of the gospel of peace;</u> Above all, <u>taking the shield of faith</u>, wherewith ye shall be able to quench all the fiery darts of the wicked. And <u>take the helmet of salvation</u>, and <u>the sword of the Spirit, which is the word of God</u>: <u>Praying always</u> with all prayer and supplication in the Spirit, and watching thereunto with all perseverance and supplication for all saints; And for me, that utterance may be given unto me, that I may open my mouth boldly, to make known the mystery of the gospel, For which I am an ambassador in bonds: that therein I may speak boldly, as I ought to speak. But that ye also may know my affairs, and how I do, Tychicus, a beloved brother and faithful minister in the Lord, shall make known to you all things: Whom I have sent unto you for the same purpose, that ye might know our affairs, and that he might comfort your hearts. Peace be to the brethren, and love with faith, from God the Father and the Lord Jesus Christ. <u>Grace be with all them that love our Lord Jesus Christ in sincerity.</u> Amen. Ephesians 6

In his second letter to Timothy, Paul knows his time is short and he states:

I have fought a good fight, I have finished my course, <u>I have kept the faith</u>: Henceforth there is laid up for me a crown of righteousness, which the Lord, the righteous judge, shall give me at that day: and not to me only, <u>but unto all them also that love his appearing</u>. 2 Timothy 4:7, 8

When I consider this amazing man, I am reminded of the words of Jesus:

And they were astonished out of measure, saying among themselves, Who then can be saved? And Jesus looking upon them saith, With men it is impossible, but not with God: for <u>with God all things are possible</u>. Mark 10:26, 27

These are words that should bring great hope to every believer!

Heavenly Father, I want to thank You for this beloved apostle and for the priceless gift of the True Gospel of Jesus Christ that You gave to us through him. My Father, please grant me the heart of Jesus and the passion for knowing him that Paul so fervently desired. Fill me with an ever more loving, merciful, kind, longsuffering, and gentle spirit as Your Holy Spirit bears good fruit through me to heal the brokenhearted and give hope to the despairing and the lost. Thank You, Father, for sending Jesus to save me and keep me. Thank You, Jesus, for loving me so much that You laid down your life so that I could live. Please hold me close Jesus and walk with me all the days of my life. Amen.

Chapter 8

THE ULTIMATE DECEPTION

This is my beloved Son, in whom I am well pleased; hear ye him.
Matthew 17:5

The first book of the Bible tells us about a man who lived a long time ago; one to whom God revealed Himself and gave a very special promise. In doing so, a covenant (solemn binding agreement) was established between the two that would have an unparalleled impact on the lives of every human who ever lived! This agreement, as in any contract, spelled out the terms and conditions for fulfillment very specifically. It also spelled out the extraordinary benefits that would result from obedience to the terms of the agreement. From this interaction, we begin to comprehend the awesome wisdom of God, as He reveals His plan and purpose for each one of us, and we begin to realize how unsurpassable His love is for us!

And when Abram was ninety years old and nine, the LORD appeared to Abram, and said unto him, I am the Almighty God; <u>walk before me, and be thou perfect</u>. And <u>I will make my covenant between me and thee</u>, and will multiply thee exceedingly. And Abram fell on his face: and God talked with him, saying, As for me, behold, <u>my covenant is with thee</u>, and <u>thou shalt be a father of many nations</u>. Neither shall thy name any more be called Abram, but <u>thy name shall be Abraham;</u>

for a father of many nations have I made thee. And I will make thee exceeding fruitful, and **I will make nations of thee**, and **kings shall come out of thee**. And I will establish my covenant between me and thee and **thy seed after thee in their generations for an everlasting covenant**, to be a God unto thee, and to thy seed after thee. And I will give unto thee, and to thy seed after thee, the land wherein thou art a stranger, all the land of Canaan, for an everlasting possession; and I will be their God. And God said unto Abraham, Thou shalt keep my covenant therefore, thou, and thy seed after thee in their generations. This is my covenant, which ye shall keep, between me and you and thy seed after thee; Every man child among you shall be circumcised. And ye shall **circumcise** the flesh of your foreskin; and it shall be a token of the covenant betwixt me and you. And he that is eight days old shall be circumcised among you, every man child in your generations, he that is born in the house, or bought with money of any stranger, which is not of thy seed. He that is born in thy house, and he that is bought with thy money, must needs be circumcised: and my covenant shall be in your flesh for an everlasting covenant. And the uncircumcised man child whose flesh of his foreskin is not circumcised, that soul shall be cut off from his people; he hath broken my covenant. And God said unto Abraham, As for Sarai thy wife, thou shalt not call her name Sarai, but Sarah shall her name be. And I will bless her, and **give thee a son also of her**: yea, I will bless her, and she shall be **a mother of nations**; kings of people shall be of her. **Genesis 17:1-16**

The root word in the Hebrew language for "Covenant" is berith, which means "to cut," and so a covenant is a cutting. What is symbolized by this is the serious and solemn nature of the agreement in that it is sealed by shed blood. In this particular covenant, the seal is the circumcision of every male under the agreement.

"In the Old Testament a spiritual idea is attached to circumcision. It was the symbol of purity (Isa. 52:1). We read of uncircumcised lips (Ex. 6:12, 30), ears (Jer. 6:10), hearts (Lev. 26:41). The fruit of a tree that is unclean is spoken of as uncircumcised (Lev. 19:23). It was a sign and seal of the covenant of grace as well as of the national covenant between God and the Hebrews. (1.) It sealed the promises made to Abraham, which related to the commonwealth of Israel, national promises. (2.) But the promises made to Abraham included the promise of redemption (Gal. 3:14), a promise which has come upon us. The covenant with Abraham was a dispensation or a specific form of the covenant of grace, and circumcision was a sign and seal of that covenant. It had a spiritual meaning. It signified purification of the heart, inward circumcision effected by the Spirit (Deut. 10:16; 30:6; Ezek. 44:7; Acts 7:51; Rom. 2:28; Col. 2:11). Circumcision as a symbol shadowing forth sanctification by the Holy Spirit has now given way to the symbol of baptism (q.v.). But the truth embodied in both ordinances is ever the same, the removal of sin, the sanctifying effects of grace in the heart. Under the Jewish dispensation, church and state were identical. No one could be a member of the one without also being a member of the other. Circumcision was a sign and seal of membership in both. Every circumcised person bore thereby evidence that he was one of the chosen people, a member of the church of God as it then existed, and consequently also a member of the Jewish commonwealth." *www.kingjamesonlinebible.org*

So, we learn here that God has made an amazing promise to Abraham and his wife, Sarah. He states that, through them, ALL nations will be blessed. Despite the fact that Sarah is beyond the age of child-bearing, she will give birth to a son from whom many nations will be made! It is nothing short of a miraculous promise and both Abraham and Sarah have a hard time believing it (see Genesis 17, 18). Never the less, the promise is fulfilled with the birth of a son who is aptly named Isaac, which means "Laughter."

And the LORD visited Sarah as he had said, and the LORD did unto Sarah as he had spoken. For Sarah conceived, and bare Abraham a son in his old age, at the set time of which God had spoken to him. And Abraham called the name of his son that was born unto him, whom Sarah bare to him, Isaac. And Abraham circumcised his son Isaac being eight days old, as God had commanded him. And Abraham was an hundred years old, when his son Isaac was born unto him. And Sarah said, God hath made me to laugh, so that all that hear will laugh with me. And she said, Who would have said unto Abraham, that Sarah should have given children suck? for I have born him a son in his old age. Genesis 21:1-7

It was not too many years after this joyful event that God gave Abraham a new command; one which portended a terrible tragedy for this family!

And it came to pass after these things, that God did tempt Abraham, and said unto him, Abraham: and he said, Behold, here I am. And he said, Take now thy son, thine only son Isaac, whom thou lovest, and get thee into the land of Moriah; and offer him there for a burnt offering upon one of the mountains which I will tell thee of. Genesis 22:1, 2

What was that? Did God just order Abraham to sacrifice his only son; the one from whom many nations were to come from? What about the promises He made? How is it right to kill his only son by his own hand under ANY circumstance? How is Sarah to know? What about Isaac? Why some mountain in Moriah three

152

days distant? How could there be any possible justification for doing this?

I am certain that these and many other questions were tormenting the mind of Abraham as he spent the longest three days of his life journeying with Isaac to the place where God told him to go to perform the sacrifice. As a father myself, I can empathize with Abraham as he wrestled with the worst nightmare scenario of his life! What could worse than the death of your child? How is it possible, knowing that it was by your own hand?

And Abraham rose up early in the morning, and saddled his ass, and took two of his young men with him, and Isaac his son, and clave the wood for the burnt offering, and rose up, and went unto the place of which God had told him. Then on the third day Abraham lifted up his eyes, and saw the place afar off. And Abraham said unto his young men, Abide ye here with the ass; and I and the lad will go yonder and worship, and come again to you. And Abraham took the wood of the burnt offering, and laid it upon Isaac his son; and he took the fire in his hand, and a knife; and they went both of them together. And Isaac spake unto Abraham his father, and said, My father: and he said, Here am I, my son. And he said, Behold the fire and the wood: but where is the lamb for a burnt offering? And Abraham said, My son, God will provide himself a lamb for a burnt offering: so they went both of them together. And they came to the place which God had told him of; and Abraham built an altar there, and laid the wood in order, and bound Isaac his son, and laid him on the altar upon the wood. Genesis 22:3-9

Remember dear reader, that there are no accidents with God. We are now at the moment of truth for Abraham. Does he love God more than Isaac? Or, does he love Isaac more than God?

And Abraham stretched forth his hand, and took the knife to slay his son. Genesis 22:10

Abraham has made his choice. It is a moment of supreme faith in God, as Abraham believed that God would fulfill ALL His promises that were made, even if it meant He had to raise Isaac up from the dead! We see this recorded in the New Testament:

By faith Abraham, when he was tried, offered up Isaac: and he that had received the promises offered up his only begotten son, Of whom it was said, That in Isaac shall thy seed be called: <u>Accounting that God was able to raise him up, even from the dead</u>; from whence also he received him in a figure. Hebrews 11:17-19

As we conclude this dramatic story in the book of Genesis, we come to learn more about who God is and what He expects of us.

And the angel of the LORD called unto him out of heaven, and said, Abraham, Abraham: and he said, Here am I. And he said, Lay not thine hand upon the lad, neither do thou any thing unto him: <u>for now I know that thou fearest God</u>, seeing thou hast not withheld thy son, thine only son from me. And Abraham lifted up his eyes, and looked, and behold behind him a ram caught in a thicket by his horns: and Abraham went and took the ram, and offered him up for a burnt offering in the stead of his son. And Abraham called the name of that place Jehovahjireh (God will provide)**: as it is said to this day, In the mount of the LORD it shall be seen. And the angel of the LORD called unto Abraham out of heaven the second time, And said, By myself have I sworn, saith the LORD, for because thou hast done this thing, and hast not withheld thy son, thine only son: That in blessing I will bless thee, and in multiplying I will multiply thy seed as the stars of the heaven, and as the sand**

which is upon the sea shore; and thy seed shall possess the gate of his enemies; And in thy seed shall all the nations of the earth be blessed; <u>because thou hast obeyed my voice</u>. Genesis 22:11-18

So, what was God teaching us in this history changing story? We read that God had a plan all along and that His plan would reach its' ultimate fulfillment in the person of HIS only son! This event foreshadows the future final sacrifice for all of us! We learn that it is by faith in God and reverent fear in Him that He is pleased and will bless us. We learn that we must love God more than anything in this world; including our own children, as well as ourselves. We learn that through Abraham's obedience to the voice of God, ALL nations of the earth would be blessed. We learn that God is full of tender mercy, is faithful, and will provide the sacrifice. One day, another Son will be sacrificed at the same location that God told Abraham to sacrifice Isaac - the site of the first and second temple in Jerusalem; also known as the "Temple Mount." God is teaching us the way of hope, truth, and life!

Throughout the Old Testament, God spoke through men by His Holy Spirit and taught us about the coming of the future Savior or Messiah. What is the definition of the word, Messiah?

"Messiah (Heb. mashiah), in all the thirty-nine instances of its' occurring in the Old Testament, is rendered by the LXX. Christos. It means anointed. Thus <u>priests</u> (Ex. 28:41; 40:15; Num. 3:3), <u>prophets</u> (1 Kings 19:16), and <u>kings</u> (1 Sam. 9:16; 16:3; 2 Sam. 12:7) were anointed with oil, and so consecrated to their respective offices. The great Messiah is anointed 'above his fellows' (Ps. 45:7); i.e., <u>he embraces in himself all the three offices</u>." *www.kingjamesonline.org*

155

Let us look at some of the many Old Testament Prophecies regarding the identity of the Messiah and Savior of the world, as well as their corresponding New Testament Scriptures. Remember, dear reader, these prophetic words in the Old Testament were written and recorded hundreds, and some thousands, of years in advance of the birth of Jesus Christ and they have ALL been fulfilled in Him! I encourage you, dear reader, to have your Bible open as you go through these Scriptures. The proof is here for every ear that will hear and every eye that will see; Jesus is the Savior of all mankind!

His pre-existence	Micah 5:2	John 1:1, 14
Born of the seed of a woman	Genesis 3:15	Matthew 1:18
Of the seed of Abraham	Genesis 12:3	Matthew 1:1-16
All nations blessed by Abraham's seed	Genesis 12:3	Matthew 8:5, 10
God would provide Himself a Lamb as an offering	Genesis 22:8	John 1:29
From the tribe of Judah	Genesis 49:10	Matthew 1:1-3
Heir to the throne of David	Isaiah 9:6-7	Matthew 1:1
Born in Bethlehem	Micah 5:2	Matthew 2:1
Born of a virgin	Isaiah 7:14	Matthew 1:18
His name is Immanuel - "God	Isaiah 7:14	Matthew 1:23

with us"

Declared to be the Son of God	Psalm 2:7	Matthew 3:17
His messenger before Him in spirit of Elijah	Malachi 4:5-6	Luke 1:17
Preceded by a messenger to prepare His way	Malachi 3:1	Matthew 11:7-11
Messenger crying "Prepare ye the way of the Lord"	Isaiah 40:3	Matthew 3:3
Would be a Prophet of the children of Israel	Deuteronomy 18:15	Matthew 2:15
Called out of Egypt	Hosea 11:1	Matthew 2:15
Slaughter of the children	Jeremiah 31:15	Matthew2:18
Would be a Nazarene	Judges 13:5; Amos 2:11; Lam. 4:7	Matthew 2:23
Brought light to Zabulon and Nephthalm, Galilee of the Gentiles	Isaiah 9:1-2	Matthew 4:15
Presented with gifts	Psalm 72:10	Matthew 2:1, 11
Rejected by His own	Isaiah 53:3	Luke 9:22
He is the stone which the	Psalm 118:22-	Matthew

builders rejected which became the headstone	23; Isaiah 28:16	21:42; 1 Peter 2:7
A stone of stumbling to Israel	Isaiah 8:14-15	1 Peter 2:8
Betrayed by a friend	Psalms 41:9	John 13:21
Sold for 30 pieces of silver	Zechariah 11:12	Matthew 26:15; Luke 22:5
The 30 pieces of silver given for the potter's field	Zechariah 11:12	Matthew 27:9-10
The 30 pieces of silver thrown in the temple	Zechariah 11:13	Matthew 27:5
Forsaken by His disciples	Zechariah 13:7	Matthew 26:56
Accused by false witnesses	Psalm 35:11	Matthew 26:60
Silent to accusations	Isaiah 53:7	Matthew 27:14
Healed the blind/deaf/lame/dumb	Isaiah 35:5-6; Isaiah 29:18	Matthew 11:5
Preached to the poor/brokenhearted/captives	Isaiah 61:1	Matthew 11:5
Came to bring a sword, not peace	Micah 7:6	Matthew 10:34-35
He bore our sickness	Isaiah 53:4	Matthew 8:16-

Spat upon, smitten and scourged	Isaiah 50:6, 53:5	Matthew 27:26, 30
Smitten on the cheek	Micah 5:1	Matthew 27:30
Hated without a cause	Psalm 35:19	Matthew 27:23
The sacrificial lamb	Isaiah 53:5	John 1:29
Given for a COVENANT	Isaiah 42:6; Jeremiah 31:31-34	Romans 11:27; Galatians 3:17, 4:24; Hebrews 8:6, 8, 10; 10:16, 29; 12:24; 13:20
Would not strive or cry	Isaiah 42:2, 3	Mark 7:36
People would hear not and see not	Isaiah 6:9-10	Matthew 13:14, 15
People trust in traditions of men	Isaiah 29:13	Matthew 15:9
People give God lip service	Isaiah 29:13	Matthew 15:8
God delights in Him	Isaiah 42:1	Matthew 3:17, 17:5
Wounded for our sins	Isaiah 53:5	John 6:51
He bore the sins of many	Isaiah 53:10-12	Mark 10:45

Messiah not killed for Himself	Daniel 9:26	Matthew 20:28
Gentiles flock to Him	Isaiah 55:5, 60:3, 65:1; Malachi 1:11;2 Samuel 22:44, 45; Psalm 2:7, 8	Matthew 8:10
Crucified with criminals	Isaiah 53:12	Matthew 27:35
His body was pierced	Zechariah 12:10; Psalm 22:16	John 20:25, 27
Thirsty during execution	Psalm 22:15	John 19:28
Given vinegar and gall for thirst	Psalm 69:21	Matthew 27:34
Soldiers gambled for his garment	Psalm 22:18	Matthew 27:35
People mocked, "He trusted in God, let Him deliver him!"	Psalm 22:7, 8	Matthew 27:43
People sat there looking at Him	Psalm 22:17	Matthew 27:36
Cried, "My God, my God why hast thou forsaken me?"	Psalm 22:1	Matthew 27:46
Darkness over the land	Amos 8:9	Matthew 27:45

No bones broken	Psalm 34:20; Numbers 9:12	John 19:33-36
Side pierced	Zechariah 12:10	John 19:34
Buried with the rich	Isaiah 53:9	Matthew 27:57, 60
Resurrected from the dead	Psalm 16:10, 11; 49:15	Mark 16:6
Priest after the order of Melchizedek	Psalm 110:4	Hebrews 5:5, 6; 6:20; 7:15- 17
Ascended to right hand of God	Psalm 68:18	Luke 24:51
LORD said unto Him, "Sit thou at my right hand, until I make thine enemies thy footstool"	Psalm 110:1	Matt 22:44; Mark 12:36; 16:19; Luke 20:42, 43; Acts 2:34, 35; Hebrews 1:13

Beloved ones searching for the truth, the very first book of the New Testament records the fulfillment of God's promises to Abraham for all generations of believers. We learn exactly who the Messiah is!

The book of the generation of <u>Jesus Christ</u>, the son of David, the son of <u>Abraham</u>. Abraham begat Isaac; and Isaac begat Jacob; and Jacob begat Judas and his brethren; And Judas

begat Phares and Zara of Thamar; and Phares begat Esrom; and Esrom begat Aram; And Aram begat Aminadab; and Aminadab begat Naasson; and Naasson begat Salmon; And Salmon begat Booz of Rachab; and Booz begat Obed of Ruth; and Obed begat Jesse; And Jesse begat David the king; and David the king begat Solomon of her that had been the wife of Urias; And Solomon begat Roboam; and Roboam begat Abia; and Abia begat Asa; And Asa begat Josaphat; and Josaphat begat Joram; and Joram begat Ozias; And Ozias begat Joatham; and Joatham begat Achaz; and Achaz begat Ezekias; And Ezekias begat Manasses; and Manasses begat Amon; and Amon begat Josias; And Josias begat Jechonias and his brethren, about the time they were carried away to Babylon: And after they were brought to Babylon, Jechonias begat Salathiel; and Salathiel begat Zorobabel; And Zorobabel begat Abiud; and Abiud begat Eliakim; and Eliakim begat Azor; And Azor begat Sadoc; and Sadoc begat Achim; and Achim begat Eliud; And Eliud begat Eleazar; and Eleazar begat Matthan; and Matthan begat Jacob; And Jacob begat Joseph the husband of Mary, of whom was born <u>Jesus, who is called Christ</u>. So all the generations from Abraham to David are fourteen generations; and from David until the carrying away into Babylon are fourteen generations; and from the carrying away into Babylon unto Christ are fourteen generations. Now the birth of <u>Jesus Christ</u> was on this wise: When as his mother Mary was espoused to Joseph, before they came together, she was found with child of the Holy Ghost. Then Joseph her husband, being a just man, and not willing to make her a public example, was minded to put her away privily. But while he thought on these things, behold, the angel of the LORD appeared unto him in a dream, saying, Joseph, thou son of David, fear not to take unto thee Mary thy wife: <u>for that which is conceived in her is of the Holy Ghost. And she shall bring forth a son, and thou shalt call his name JESUS: for he shall</u>

save his people from their sins. Now all this was done, that it might be fulfilled which was spoken of the Lord by the prophet, saying, Behold, a virgin shall be with child, and shall bring forth a son, <u>and they shall call his name Emmanuel, which being interpreted is, God with us</u>. Then Joseph being raised from sleep did as the angel of the Lord had bidden him, and took unto him his wife: And knew her not till she had brought forth her firstborn son: and he called his name JESUS. Matthew 1

After Jesus was betrayed, arrested, tried, judged, executed on a cross, and resurrected three days later, it would be an understatement to say that the populace Jerusalem and surrounding area were in a state of shock! Two of His followers were going home after these tumultuous events and this is what happened along the way:

And, behold, two of them went that same day to a village called Emmaus, which was from Jerusalem about threescore furlongs. And they talked together of all these things which had happened. And it came to pass, that, while they communed together and reasoned, <u>Jesus himself</u> drew near, and went with them. But their eyes were holden that they should not know him. And he said unto them, What manner of communications are these that ye have one to another, as ye walk, and are sad? And the one of them, whose name was Cleopas, answering said unto him, Art thou only a stranger in Jerusalem, and hast not known the things which are come to pass there in these days? And he said unto them, What things? And they said unto him, <u>Concerning Jesus of Nazareth</u>, which was a prophet mighty in deed and word before God and all the people: And how the chief priests and our rulers delivered him to be condemned to death, and have crucified him. But we trusted that it had been he which should have redeemed Israel: and beside all this, to

day is the third day since these things were done. Yea, and certain women also of our company made us astonished, which were early at the sepulchre; And when they found not his body, they came, saying, that they had also seen a vision of angels, which said that he was alive. And certain of them which were with us went to the sepulchre, and found it even so as the women had said: but him they saw not. Then he said unto them, <u>O fools, and slow of heart to believe all that the prophets have spoken</u>: Ought not Christ to have suffered these things, and to enter into his glory? <u>And beginning at Moses and all the prophets, he expounded unto them in all the scriptures the things concerning himself</u>. And they drew nigh unto the village, whither they went: and he made as though he would have gone further. But they constrained him, saying, Abide with us: for it is toward evening, and the day is far spent. And he went in to tarry with them. And it came to pass, as he sat at meat with them, he took bread, and blessed it, and brake, and gave to them. And their eyes were opened, and they knew him; and he vanished out of their sight. And they said one to another, <u>Did not our heart burn within us</u>, while he talked with us by the way, <u>and while he opened to us the scriptures</u>? Luke 24:13-32

Dear reader, does not your heart burn within you upon learning the truth of Jesus and having read the Scriptures in a new light?

Below are hundreds of prophetic Scriptures in both the Old and New Testament that point to ONE, and only ONE who will fulfill all of them as THE Prophet of prophets, THE Priest of priests, and THE King of kings! I <u>strongly</u> encourage you to look up these Scriptures for yourselves, dear readers. This is the truth:

Genesis 9:26, 27...The God of Shem will be the Son of Shem...Luke 3:36
Genesis 12:3...As Abraham's seed, will bless all nations...Acts

164

3:25, 26

Genesis 12:7...The Promise made to Abraham's Seed...Galatians 3:16

Genesis 14:18...A priest after Melchizedek...Hebrews 6:20

Genesis 14:18...A King also…Hebrews 7:2

Genesis 14:18...The Last Supper foreshadowed...Matthew 26:26-29

Genesis 17:19...The Seed of Isaac...Romans 9:7

Genesis 22:8...The Lamb of God promised...John 1:29

Genesis 22:18...As Isaac's seed, will bless all nations...Galatians 3:16

Genesis 26:2-5...The Seed of Isaac promised as the Redeemer...Hebrews 11:18

Genesis 49:10...The time of His coming...Luke 2:1-7; Galatians 4:4

Genesis 49:10...The Seed of Judah...Luke 3:33

Genesis 49:10...Called Shiloh or One Sent....John 17:3

Genesis 49:10...To come before Judah lost identity....John 11:47-52

Genesis 49:10...To Him shall the obedience of the people be....John 10:16

Exodus 3:13,14...The Great "I Am"...John 4:26

Exodus 12:5...A Lamb without blemish...1 Peter 1:19

Exodus 12:13...The blood of the Lamb saves from wrath...Romans 5:8

Exodus 12:21-27...Christ is our Passover...1 Corinthians 5;7

Exodus 12:46...Not a bone of the Lamb to be broken....John 19:31-36

Exodus 15:2...His exaltation predicted as Yeshua (Joshua – God saves)...Acts 7:55, 56

Exodus 15:11...His Character-Holiness...Luke 1:35; Acts 4:27

Exodus 17:6...The Spiritual Rock of Israel...1 Corinthians 10;4

Exodus 33:19...His Character-Merciful...Luke 1:72

Leviticus 14:11...The leper cleansed-Sign to priesthood...Luke

5:12-14; Acts 6:7

Leviticus 16:15-17...Prefigures Christ's once-for-all death...Hebrews 9:7-14

Leviticus 16:27...Suffering outside the Camp...Matthew 27:33; Hebrews 13:11, 12

Leviticus 17:11...The Blood-the life of the flesh...Matthew 26:28; Mark 10:45

Leviticus 17:11...It is the blood that makes atonement...1 John 3:14-18

Leviticus 23:36-37...The Drink-offering: "If any man thirst." ...John 19:31-36

Numbers 9:12...Not a bone of Him broken...John 19:31-36

Numbers 21:9...The serpent on a pole-Christ lifted up...John 3:14-18

Numbers 24:17...Time: "I shall see him, but not now."...Galatians 4:4

Deuteronomy 18:15..."This is of a truth that prophet."...John 6:14

Deuteronomy 18:15-16..."Had ye believed Moses, ye would believe me."...John 5:45-47

Deuteronomy 18:18...Sent by the Father to speak His word...John 8:28, 29

Deuteronomy 18:19...Whoever will not hear must bear his sin...John 12:15

Deuteronomy 21:23...Cursed is he that hangs on a tree...Galatians 3:10-13

Ruth 4:4-9...Christ, our kinsman, has redeemed us...Ephesians 1:3-7

1 Samuel 2:10...Shall be an anointed King to the Lord...Matthew 28:18; John 12:15

2 Samuel 7:12...David's Seed...Matthew 1:1

2 Samuel 7:14a...The Son of God...Luke 1:32

2 Samuel 7:16...David's house established forever...Luke 3:31; Revelation 22:16

2 Kings 2:11...The bodily ascension to heaven illustrated...Luke 24:51

1 Chronicles 17:11...David's Seed...Matthew 1:1, 9:27

1 Chronicles 17:12, 13...To reign on David's throne forever...Luke 1:32, 33

1 Chronicles 17:13..."I will be His Father, He...my Son."...Hebrews 1:5

Job 19:23-27...The Resurrection predicted...John 5:24-29

Psalm 2:1-3...The enmity of kings foreordained...Acts 4:25-28

Psalm 2:2...To own the title, Anointed (Christ)...Acts 2:36

Psalm 2:6...His Character-Holiness...John 8:46; Revelation 3:7

Psalm 2:6...To own the title King...Matthew 2:2

Psalm 2:7...Declared the Beloved Son...Matthew 3:17

Psalm 2:7, 8...The Crucifixion and Resurrection intimated...Acts 13:29-33

Psalm 2:12...Life comes through faith in Him...John 20:31

Psalm 8:2...The mouths of babes perfect His praise...Matthew 21:16

Psalm 8:5, 6...His humiliation and exaltation...Luke 24:50-53; 1 Corinthians 15:27

Psalm 16:10...Was not to see corruption...Acts 2:31

Psalm 16:9-11...Was to arise from the dead...John 20:9

Psalm 17:15...The resurrection predicted...Luke 24:6

Psalm 22:1...Forsaken because of sins of others...2 Corinthians 5:21

Psalm 22:1...Words spoken from Calvary, "My God..." Mark 15:34

Psalm 22:2...Darkness upon Calvary...Matthew 27:45

Psalm 22:7...They shoot out the lip and shake the head...Matthew 27:39

Psalm 22:8..He trusted in God, let Him deliver Him"...Matthew 27:43

Psalm 22:9...Born the Saviour...Luke 2:7

Psalm 22:14...Died of a broken (ruptured) heart...John 19:34

Psalm 22:14, 15...Suffered agony on Calvary...Mark 15:34-37

Psalm 22:15...He thirsted....John 19:28

Psalm 22:16...They pierced His hands and His feet...John 19:34, 37, 20:27

Psalm 22:17, 18...Stripped Him before the stares of men...Luke 23:34, 35

Psalm 22:18...They parted His garments...John 19:23, 24

Psalm 22:20, 21...He committed Himself to God...Luke 23:46

Psalm 22:20, 21...Satanic power bruising the Redeemer's heel...Hebrews 2:14

Psalm 22:22...His Resurrection declared....John 20:17

Psalm 22:27...He shall be the governor of the nations...Colossians 1:16

Psalm 22:31..."It is finished"....John 19:30

Psalm 23:1...."I am the Good Shepherd".....John 10:11

Psalm 24:3...His exaltation predicted...Acts 1:11; Philemon 2:9

Psalm 30:3....His resurrection predicted...Acts 2:32

Psalm 31:5..."Into thy hands I commit my spirit"...Luke 23:46

Psalm 31:11...His acquaintances fled from Him...Mark 14:50

Psalm 31:13...They took counsel to put Him to death...John 11:53

Psalm 31:14, 15..." He trusted in God, let Him deliver him"...Matthew 27:43

Psalm 34:20...Not a bone of Him broken...John 19:31-36

Psalm 35:11...False witnesses rose up against Him...Matthew 26:59

Psalm 35:19...He was hated without a cause...John 15:25

Psalm 38:11...His friends stood afar off...Luke 23:49

Psalm 40:2-5...The joy of His resurrection predicted...John 20:20

Psalm 40:6-8...His delight-the will of the Father...John 4:34

Psalm 40:9...He was to preach the Righteousness in Israel...Matthew 4:17

Psalm 40:14...Confronted by adversaries in the Garden....John

18:4-6

Psalm 41:9...Betrayed by a familiar friend...John 13:18

Psalm 45:2...Words of Grace come from His lips...Luke 4:22

Psalm 45:6...To own the title, God or Elohim...Hebrews 1:8

Psalm 45:7...A special anointing by the Holy Spirit...Matthew 3:16; Hebrews 1:9

Psalm 45:7, 8...Called the Christ (Messiah or Anointed)...Luke 2:11

Psalm 55:12-14...Betrayed by a friend, not an enemy....John 13:18

Psalm 55:15...Unrepentant death of the Betrayer...Matthew 27:3-5; Acts 1:16-19

Psalm 68:18...To give gifts to men...Ephesians 4:7-16

Psalm 68:18...Ascended into Heaven...Luke 24:51

Psalm 69:4...Hated without a cause...John 15:25

Psalm 69:8...A stranger to own brethren...Luke 8:20, 21

Psalm 69:9...Zealous for the Lord's House...John 2:17

Psalm 69:14-20...Messiah's anguish of soul before crucifixion...Matthew 26:36-45

Psalm 69:20..."My soul is exceeding sorrowful."...Matthew 26:38

Psalm 69:21...Given vinegar in thirst...Matthew 27:34

Psalm 69:26...The Savior given and smitten by God...John 17:4; 18:11

Psalm 72:10, 11...Great persons were to visit Him...Matthew 2:1-11

Psalm 72:16...The corn of wheat to fall into the Ground....John 12:24

Psalm 72:17...All nations shall be blessed by Him...Acts 2:11, 12, 41

Psalm 78:1.2...He would teach in parables...Matthew 13:34-35

Psalm 78:2...To speak the Wisdom of God with authority...Matthew 7:29

Psalm 88:8...They stood afar off and watched...Luke 23:49

Psalm 89:27...Emmanuel to be higher than earthly kings...Luke 1:32, 33

Psalm 89:35-37...David's Seed, throne, kingdom endure forever...Luke 1:32, 33

Psalm 89:36-37...His character-Faithfulness...Revelation 1:5

Psalm 90:2...He is from everlasting (Micah 5:2)...John 1:1

Psalm 91:11, 12...Identified as Messianic; used to tempt Christ...Luke 4:10, 11

Psalm 97:9...His exaltation predicted...Acts 1:11; Ephesians 1:20

Psalm 100:5...His character-Goodness...Matthew 19:16, 17

Psalm 102:1-11...The Suffering and Reproach of Calvary...John 21:16-30

Psalm 102:25-27...Messiah is the Pre-existent Son...Hebrews 1:10-12

Psalm 109:25...Ridiculed...Matthew 27:39

Psalm 110:1...Son of David...Matthew 22:43

Psalm 110:1...To ascend to the right-hand of the Father...Mark 16:19

Psalm 110:1...David's son called Lord...Matthew 22:44, 45

Psalm 110:4...A priest after Melchizedek's order...Hebrews 6:20

Psalm 112:4...His character-Compassionate, Gracious, et al...Matthew 9:36

Psalm 118:17, 18...Messiah's Resurrection assured...Luke 24:5-7; 1 Corinthians 15:20

Psalm 118:22, 23...The rejected stone is Head of the corner...Matthew 21:42, 43

Psalm 118:26...The Blessed One presented to Israel...Matthew 21:9

Psalm 118:26...To come while Temple standing...Matthew 21:12-15

Psalm 132:11...The Seed of David (the fruit of His Body)...Luke 1:32

Psalm 138:1-6...The supremacy of David's Seed amazes kings...Matthew 2:2-6

Psalm 147:3, 6...The earthly ministry of Christ described...Luke 4:18

Psalm 1:23...He will send the Spirit of God... John 16:7

Song of Solomon 5:16...The altogether lovely One...John 1:17

Isaiah 6:1...When Isaiah saw His glory... John 12:40, 41

Isaiah 6:9-10...Parables fall on deaf ears...Matthew 13:13-15

Isaiah 6:9-12...Blinded to Christ and deaf to His words...Acts 28:23-29

Isaiah 7:14...To be born of a virgin...Luke 1:35

Isaiah 7:14...To be Emmanuel-God with us...Matthew 1:18-23

Isaiah 8:8...Called Emmanuel...Matthew 28:20

Isaiah 8:14...A stone of stumbling, a Rock of offense... 1 Pet. 2:8

Isaiah 9:1, 2...His ministry to begin in Galilee...Matthew 4:12-17

Isaiah 9:6...A child born-Humanity...Luke 1:31

Isaiah 9:6...A Son given-Deity...Luke 1:32; John 1:14; 1 Timothy 3:16

Isaiah 9:6...Declared to be the Son of God with power... Romans 1:3, 4

Isaiah 9:6...The Wonderful One...Luke 4:22

Isaiah 9:6...The Counselor...Matthew 13:54

Isaiah 9:6...The Mighty God...Matthew 11:20

Isaiah 9:6...The Everlasting Father...John 8:58

Isaiah 9:6...The Prince of Peace...John 16:33

Isaiah 9:7...To establish an everlasting kingdom...Luke 1:32-33

Isaiah 9:7...His Character-Just...John 5:30

Isaiah 9:7...No end to his Government, Throne, and Peace...Luke 1:32-33

Isaiah 11:1...Called a Nazarene-the Branch...Matthew 2:23

Isaiah 11:1...A rod out of Jesse-Son of Jesse...Luke 3:23, 32

Isaiah 11:2...The anointed One by the Spirit...Matthew 3:16, 17

Isaiah 11:2...His Character-Wisdom, Understanding, et al...John 4:4-26

Isaiah 11:4...His Character-Truth...John 14:6

Isaiah 11:10...The Gentiles seek Him...John 12:18-21

Isaiah 12:2...Called Jesus-Yeshua...Matthew 1:21

Isaiah 25:8...The Resurrection predicted...I Corinthians 15:54

Isaiah 26:19...His power of Resurrection predicted...John 11:43, 44

Isaiah 28:16...The Messiah is the precious corner stone...Acts 4:11, 12

Isaiah 29:13...He indicated hypocritical obedience to His Word...Matthew 15:7-9

Isaiah 29:14...The wise are confounded by the Word...I Corinthians 1:18-31

Isaiah 32:2...A Refuge-A man shall be a hiding place...Matthew 23:37

Isaiah 35:4...He will come and save you...Matthew 1:21

Isaiah 35:5...To have a ministry of miracles...Matthew 11:4-6

Isaiah 40:3, 4...Preceded by forerunner...John 1:23

Isaiah 40:9..."Behold your God."...John 1:36, 19:14

Isaiah 40:11...A shepherd-compassionate life-giver...John 10:10-18

Isaiah 42:1-4...The Servant-as a faithful, patient redeemer...Matthew 12:18-21

Isaiah 42:2...Meek and lowly...Matthew 11:28-30

Isaiah 42:3...He brings hope for the hopeless...John 4

Isaiah 42:4...The nations shall wait on His teachings...John 12:20-26

Isaiah 42:6...The Light (salvation) of the Gentiles...Luke 2:32

Isaiah 42:1, 6...His is a worldwide compassion...Matthew 28:19, 20

Isaiah 42:7...Blind eyes opened...John 9:25-38

Isaiah 43:11...He is the only Savior...Acts 4:12

Isaiah 44:3...He will send the Spirit of God...John 16:7, 13

Isaiah 45:23...He will be the Judge....John 5:22; Romans 14:11

Isaiah 48:12...The First and the Last...John 1:30; Revelation 1:8, 17

Isaiah 48:17...He came as a Teacher...John 3:2

Isaiah 49:1...Called from the womb-His humanity...Matthew 1:18

Isaiah 49:5...A Servant from the womb...Luke 1:31; Philemon 2:7

Isaiah 49:6...He is Salvation for Israel...Luke 2:29-32

Isaiah 49:6...He is the Light of the Gentiles...Acts 13:47

Isaiah 49:6...He is Salvation unto the ends of the earth...Acts 15:7-18

Isaiah 49:7...He is despised of the Nation...John 8:48-49

Isaiah 50:3...Heaven is clothed in black at His humiliation...Luke 23:44, 45

Isaiah 50:4...He is a learned counselor for the weary...Matthew 11:28, 29

Isaiah 50:5...The Servant bound willingly to obedience...Matthew 26:39

Isaiah 50:6..."I gave my back to the smiters."...Matthew 27:26

Isaiah 50:6...He was smitten on the cheeks...Matthew 26:67

Isaiah 50:6...He was spat upon...Matthew 27:30

Isaiah 52:7...To publish good tidings of peace...Luke 4:14, 15

Isaiah 52:13...The Servant exalted...Acts 1:8-11; Ephesians 1:19-22

Isaiah 52:13...Behold, My Servant...Matthew 17:5; Philemon 2:5-8

Isaiah 52:14...The Servant shockingly abused...Luke 18:31-34; Matthew 26:67, 68

Isaiah 52:15...Nations startled by message of the Servant... Romans 15:18-21

Isaiah 52:15...His blood shed to make atonement for all...Revelation 1:5

Isaiah 53:1...His people would not believe Him....John 12:37, 38

Isaiah 53:2...He would grow up in a poor family...Luke 2:7

Isaiah 53:2...Appearance of an ordinary man...Philemon 2:7-8

Isaiah 53:3...Despised....Luke 4:28, 29

Isaiah 53:3...Rejected...Matthew 27:21-23

Isaiah 53:3...Great sorrow and grief...Luke 19:41, 42

Isaiah 53:3...Men hide from being associated with Him...Mark 14:50-52

Isaiah 53:4...He would have a healing ministry...Luke 6:17-19

Isaiah 53:4...He would bear the sins of the world...1 Peter 2:24

Isaiah 53:4...Thought to be cursed by God...Matthew 27:41-43

Isaiah 53:5...Bears penalty for mankind's transgressions...Luke 23:33

Isaiah 53:5...His sacrifice would provide peace between man and God...Colossians 1:20

Isaiah 53:5...His back would be whipped...Matthew 27:26

Isaiah 53:6...He would be the sin-bearer for all mankind...Galatians 1:4

Isaiah 53:6...God's will that He bear sin for all mankind...1 John 4:10

Isaiah 53:7...Oppressed and afflicted...Matthew 27:27-31

Isaiah 53:7...Silent before his accusers...Matthew 27:12-14

Isaiah 53:7...Sacrificial lamb...John 1:29

Isaiah 53:8...Confined and persecuted...Matthew 26:27-31, 47

Isaiah 53:8...He would be judged...John 18:13-22

Isaiah 53:8...Killed...Matthew 27:35

Isaiah 53:8...Dies for the sins of the world...1 John 2:2

Isaiah 53:9...Buried in a rich man's grave...Matthew 27:57

Isaiah 53:9...Innocent and had done no violence...Mark 15:3

Isaiah 53:9...No deceit in his mouth...John 18:38

Isaiah 53:10...God's will that He die for mankind...John 18:11

Isaiah 53:10...An offering for sin... Matthew 20:28

Isaiah 53:10...Resurrected and live forever...Mark 16:16

Isaiah 53:10...He would prosper...John 17:1-5

Isaiah 53:11...God fully satisfied with His suffering...John

12:27

Isaiah 53:11...God's servant...Romans 5:18-19

Isaiah 53:11...He would justify man before God...Romans 5:8-9

Isaiah 53:11...The sin-bearer for all mankind...Hebrews 9:28

Isaiah 53:12...Exalted by God because of his sacrifice...Matthew 28:18

Isaiah 53:12...He would give up his life to save mankind...Luke 23:46

Isaiah 53:12...Grouped with criminals...Luke 23:32

Isaiah 53:12...Sin-bearer for all mankind...2 Corinthians 5:21

Isaiah 53:12...Intercede to God on behalf of mankind...Luke 23:34

Isaiah 55:3...Resurrected by God...Acts 13:34

Isaiah 55:4...A witness...John 18:37

Isaiah 59:15-16...He would come to provide salvation....John 6:40

Isaiah 59:15-16...Intercessor between man and God...Matthew 10:32

Isaiah 59:20...He would come to Zion as their Redeemer...Luke 2:38

Isaiah 61:1-2...The Spirit of God upon him...Matthew 3:16, 17

Isaiah 61:1-2...The Messiah would preach the good news...Luke 4:17-21

Isaiah 61:1-2...Provide freedom from the bondage of sin and death...John 8:31, 32

Isaiah 61:1-2...Proclaim a period of grace....John 5:24

Jeremiah 23:5-6...Descendant of David...Luke 3:23, 31

Jeremiah 23:5-6...The Messiah would be God...John 13:13

Jeremiah 23:5-6...The Messiah would be both God and Man...1 Timothy 3:16

Jeremiah 31:22...Born of a virgin...Matthew 1:18-20

Jeremiah 31:31...The Messiah would be the new covenant... Matthew 26:28

Jeremiah 33:14-15...Descendant of David...Luke 3:23-31

Ezekiel 17:22-24...Descendant of David...Luke 3:23-31

Ezekiel 34:23-24...Descendant of David...Matthew 1:1

Daniel 7:13-14...He would ascend into heaven...Acts 1:9-11

Daniel 7:13-14...Highly exalted...Ephesians 1:20-22

Daniel 7:13-14...His dominion would be everlasting...Luke 1:31-33

Daniel 9:24...To make an end to sins...Galatians 1:3-5

Daniel 9:24...He would be holy...Luke 1:35

Daniel 9:25...Announced to his people 483 years (69 weeks of years), to the exact day, after the decree to rebuild the city of Jerusalem...John 12:12-13

Daniel 9:26...Killed...Matthew 27:35

Daniel 9:26...Die for the sins of the world... Hebrews 2:9

Daniel 9:26...Killed before the destruction of the temple...Matthew 27:50-51

Daniel 10:5-6...Messiah in a glorified state...Revelation 1:13-16

Hosea 13:14...He would defeat death...1 Corinthians 15:55-57

Joel 2:32...Offer salvation to all mankind...Romans 10:12-13

Micah 5:2...Born in Bethlehem...Matthew 2:1-2

Micah 5:2...God's servant...John 15:10

Micah 5:2...From everlasting...John. 8:58

Haggai 2:6-9...He would visit the second Temple...Luke 2:27-32

Haggai 2:23...Descendant of Zerubbabel...Luke 3:23-27

Zechariah 3:8...God's servant...John 17:4

Zechariah 6:12-13...Priest and King...Hebrews 8:1

Zechariah 9:9...Greeted with rejoicing in Jerusalem...Matthew 21:8-10

Zechariah 9:9...Beheld as King...John 12:12, 13

Zechariah 9:9...The Messiah would be just...John 5:30

Zechariah 9:9...The Messiah would bring salvation...Luke 19:10

Zechariah 9:9...The Messiah would be humble...Matthew 11:29

Zechariah 9:9...Presented to Jerusalem riding on a donkey...Matthew 21:6-9

Zechariah 10:4...The cornerstone...Ephesians 2:20

Zechariah 11:4-6...At His coming, Israel to have unfit leaders...Matthew 23:1-4

Zechariah 11:4-6...Rejection causes God to remove His protection...Luke 19:41-44

Zechariah 11:4-6...Rejected in favor of another king...John 19:13-15

Zechariah 11:7...Ministry to "poor," the believing remnant...Matthew 9:35-36

Zechariah 11:8...Unbelief forces Messiah to reject them...Matthew 23:33

Zechariah 11:8...Despised...Matthew 27:20

Zechariah 11:9...Stops ministering to those who rejected Him...Matthew 13:10, 11

Zechariah 11:10-11...Rejection causes God to remove protection...Luke 19:41-44

Zechariah 11:10-11...The Messiah would be God...John 14:7

Zechariah 11:12-13...Betrayed for thirty pieces of silver...Matthew 26:14-15

Zechariah 11:12-13...Rejected...Matthew 26:14, 15

Zechariah 11:12-13...30 pieces of silver thrown into the house of the Lord... Matthew 27:3-5

Zechariah 11:12-13...The Messiah would be God...John 12:45

Zechariah 12:10...The Messiah's body would be pierced...John 19:34-37

Zechariah 12:10...The Messiah would be both God and man...John 10:30

Zechariah 12:10...The Messiah would be rejected...John 1:11

Zechariah 13:7...God's will He die for mankind...John 18:11

Zechariah 13:7...A violent death...Matthew 27:35

Zechariah 13:7...Both God and man...John 14:9

Zechariah 13:7...Israel scattered as a result of rejecting Him...Matthew 26:31-56

Malachi 3:1...Messenger to prepare the way for

Messiah...Matthew 11:10
Malachi 3:1...Sudden appearance at the temple...Mark 11:15, 16
Malachi 3:1...Messenger of the new covenant...Luke 4:43
Malachi 4:5...Forerunner in the spirit of Elijah...Matthew 3:1-2
Malachi 4:6...Forerunner would turn many to righteousness...Luke 1:16-17

Regarding these prophetic Scriptures, the apostle Peter tells us:

We have also <u>a more sure word of prophecy</u>; whereunto <u>ye do well that ye take heed</u>, as unto <u>a light that shineth in a dark place</u>, until the day dawn, and the day star arise in your hearts: Knowing this first, that <u>no prophecy of the scripture is of any private interpretation</u>. For the prophecy came not in old time by the will of man: <u>but holy men of God spake as they were moved by the Holy Ghost</u>. 2 Peter 1:19-21

We have exceedingly abundant proof that Jesus is the Messiah, the Savior, and the Son of the Living God who came into the world to save mankind from death caused by sin. What are we to conclude? Any group, organization, philosophy, doctrine, teacher or authority that denies the identity of Jesus as THE only begotten Son of God who was born of a virgin by the Holy Spirit, lived a sinless life, was crucified for our sins, was raised up to life again on the third day, was seen by numerous witnesses, ascended to Heaven, now sits at the right hand of God, and will come again as King of Kings to judge the world and inherit the Kingdom prepared for Him, is operating under the spirit of error and promoting the ULTIMATE DECEPTION!

Why?

Because, dear reader, Jesus is the lynch pin which holds all of history together. He is the way, the truth, and the life. He is the only One through whom any of us can possibly be saved. He is the point on which everything concerning the past, present, and future of mankind revolves around and, without Him, there is no hope for us, no way to God, and there is no salvation!

Of all the deceptions running rampant in our world today, the greatest of all by far is the deception that God has no Son! To believe that God has no Son, after the clear and abundant evidence from innumerable prophecies, signs, wonders, miracles and witnesses is to commit the grave sin of blasphemy against the Holy Spirit and is nothing less than calling God a liar. If God has no son, than mankind is hopelessly lost to eternal destruction as a result of sin! Without the Savior, no man can be reconciled to God and our lives are nothing more than worthless vanity. We were created by God for a very real purpose, and that purpose is both enabled and fulfilled through His Son, Jesus. Who is it that benefits the most by the ultimate deception? He is the same one who tempted Adam and Eve, as well as Jesus during his forty days in the wilderness. He is still devouring souls today, as he has throughout history when men reject the truth. We are amply warned throughout the New Testament about the workers of iniquity and the spirit of error.

Now the Spirit speaketh expressly, that in the latter times <u>some shall depart from the faith</u>, <u>giving heed to seducing spirits</u>, and <u>doctrines of devils</u>; Speaking lies in hypocrisy; having their conscience seared with a hot iron; Forbidding to marry, and commanding to abstain from meats, which God hath created to be received with thanksgiving of them which believe and know the truth. 1 Timothy 4:1-13

Be sober, be vigilant; because <u>your adversary the devil, as a</u> <u>roaring lion</u>, walketh about, <u>seeking whom he may devour</u>: 1 Peter 5:8

Listen to what the apostle's Peter and John had to say to the people of Israel after the resurrection of Jesus:

And as the lame man which was healed held Peter and John, all the people ran together unto them in the porch that is called Solomon's, greatly wondering. And when Peter saw it, he answered unto the people, Ye men of Israel, why marvel ye at this? or why look ye so earnestly on us, as though by our own power or holiness we had made this man to walk? <u>The God of</u> <u>Abraham</u>, and of Isaac, and of Jacob, the God of our fathers, <u>hath glorified his Son Jesus</u>; whom ye delivered up, and denied him in the presence of Pilate, when he was determined to let him go. But ye denied <u>the Holy One and the Just</u>, and desired a murderer to be granted unto you; And killed <u>the Prince of life</u>, whom God hath raised from the dead; whereof we are witnesses. And his name through faith in his name hath made this man strong, whom ye see and know: yea, the faith which is by him hath given him this perfect soundness in the presence of you all. And now, brethren, I wot (know) that through ignorance ye did it, as did also your rulers. <u>But those things,</u> <u>which God before had shewed by the mouth of all his prophets,</u> <u>that Christ should suffer, he hath so fulfilled</u>. <u>Repent</u> ye therefore, and <u>be converted</u>, that <u>your sins may be blotted out</u>, when the times of refreshing shall come from the presence of the Lord. And he shall send <u>Jesus Christ</u>, which before was preached unto you: Whom the heaven must receive until the times of restitution of all things, <u>which God hath spoken by the</u> <u>mouth of all his holy prophets since the world began</u>. For Moses truly said unto the fathers, <u>A prophet</u> shall the Lord your God raise up unto you of your brethren, like unto me;

him shall ye hear in all things whatsoever he shall say unto you. And it shall come to pass, <u>that every soul, which will not hear that prophet, shall be destroyed from among the people</u>. Yea, and <u>all the prophets</u> from Samuel and those that follow after, as many as have spoken, have likewise foretold of these days. Ye are the children of the prophets, and of the <u>covenant</u> which God made with our fathers, <u>saying unto Abraham, And in thy seed shall all the kindreds of the earth be blessed. Unto you first God, having raised up his Son Jesus, sent him to bless you, in turning away every one of you from his iniquities</u>. Acts 3:11-26

Finally, dear reader, we have the witness of the Most High God regarding His Son, Jesus. Let us read the Scripture at the start of this chapter in the context of the event. Jesus had just taken three of His disciples up to a mountain to pray. Here is what happened:

And after six days Jesus taketh Peter, James, and John his brother, and bringeth them up into an high mountain apart, And was transfigured before them: and his face did shine as the sun, and his raiment was white as the light. And, behold, there appeared unto them Moses and Elias talking with him. Then answered Peter, and said unto Jesus, Lord, it is good for us to be here: if thou wilt, let us make here three tabernacles; one for thee, and one for Moses, and one for Elias. <u>While he yet spake, behold, a bright cloud overshadowed them: and behold a voice out of the cloud, which said, This is my beloved Son, in whom I am well pleased; hear ye him</u>. And when the disciples heard it, they fell on their face, and were sore afraid. And Jesus came and touched them, and said, Arise, and be not afraid. And when they had lifted up their eyes, they saw no man, save Jesus only. And as they came down from the mountain, Jesus charged them, saying, <u>Tell the vision to no</u>

man, until the Son of man be risen again from the dead.
Matthew 17:1-9

Listen to what Peter had to say about this event:

For we have not followed cunningly devised fables, when we made known unto you the power and coming of our Lord Jesus Christ, but were <u>eyewitnesses</u> of his majesty. For he received <u>from God the Father honour and glory, when there came such a voice to him from the excellent glory, This is my beloved Son, in whom I am well pleased</u>. And this voice which came from heaven we heard, when we were with him in the holy mount. 2 Peter 1:16-18

Peter also warns us:

But there were <u>false prophets</u> also among the people, even as there shall be <u>false teachers among you</u>, who privily shall bring in <u>damnable heresies</u>, <u>even denying the Lord that bought them</u>, and bring upon themselves swift destruction. And <u>many</u> shall follow their pernicious ways; by reason of whom <u>the way of truth shall be evil spoken of</u>. 2 Peter 1, 2

Finally, we read the words of the apostle John who makes it very clear for us:

Beloved, believe not every spirit, but try the spirits whether they are of God: because many false prophets are gone out into the world. Hereby know ye the Spirit of God: <u>Every spirit that confesseth that Jesus Christ is come in the flesh is of God</u>: And every spirit that confesseth not that Jesus Christ is come in the flesh is not of God: and <u>this is that spirit of antichrist</u>, whereof ye have heard that it should come; and even now already is it in the world. 1 John 4:1-3

Whosoever <u>believeth that Jesus is the Christ is born of God</u>: and every one that loveth him that begat loveth him also that is begotten of him. By this we know that we love the children of God, when we love God, and keep his commandments. <u>For this is the love of God, that we keep his commandments</u>: and his commandments are not grievous. For whatsoever is born of God overcometh the world: and this is the victory that overcometh the world, even our faith. <u>Who is he that overcometh the world, but he that believeth that Jesus is the Son of God?</u> This is he that came by water and blood, even <u>Jesus Christ</u>; not by water only, but by water and blood. And it is the Spirit that beareth witness, because <u>the Spirit is truth</u>. For there are three that bear record in heaven, the Father, the Word (Jesus), and the Holy Ghost: and these three are one. 1 John 5:1-7

And this is love, that we walk after his commandments. This is the commandment, That, as ye have heard from the beginning, ye should walk in it. For <u>many deceivers</u> are entered into the world, <u>who confess not that Jesus Christ is come in the flesh.</u> <u>This is a deceiver and an antichrist.</u> Look to yourselves, that we lose not those things which we have wrought, but that we receive a full reward. Whosoever transgresseth, and abideth not in the doctrine of Christ, hath not God. He that abideth in the doctrine of Christ, he hath both the Father and the Son. If there come any unto you, and bring not this doctrine, receive him not into your house, neither bid him God speed: For he that biddeth him God speed is partaker of his evil deeds. 2 John 1:6-10

Oh most high God in Heaven, I confess to You that I have walked many days of my life without faith. I have chosen to fear men more than You, and I have followed doctrines and ideas that were convenient to me and the way I wanted to live my life. Please forgive me and show me the truth of Your Son, Jesus. Fill my heart with His love and Your Holy Spirit. Protect me from all deception, I pray; especially self-deception. I thank You God for loving me and patiently waiting for me to come home to You. Please continue to have mercy on my soul and hold me close all the days of my life. In the name of Jesus I pray, amen.

Chapter 9

THE TEARS OF THE SAINTS

So also Christ glorified not himself to be made an high priest; but he that said unto him, <u>Thou art my Son</u>, to day have I begotten thee. As he saith also in another place, Thou art a priest for ever after the order of Melchisedec. Who in the days of his flesh, when he had offered up prayers and supplications with strong crying and tears unto him that was able to save him from death, and was heard in that he feared; Though he were a Son, yet learned he obedience by the things which he suffered; And being made perfect, <u>he became the author of eternal salvation unto all them that obey him</u>; Called of God an high priest after the order of Melchisedec. Hebrews 5:5-10

Dear reader, when Jesus began his public ministry, He entered into the synagogue in Nazareth and read the words of the prophet Isaiah (Isa. 61:1, 2) and this is what happened:

And Jesus returned in the power of the Spirit into Galilee: and there went out a fame of him through all the region round about. And he taught in their synagogues, being glorified of all. And he came to Nazareth, where he had been brought up: and, as his custom was, he went into the synagogue on the sabbath day, and stood up for to read. And there was delivered unto him the book of the prophet Esaias. And when he had opened the book, he found the place where it was written, <u>The Spirit of</u>

the Lord is upon me, because he hath anointed me to preach the gospel to the poor; he hath sent me to heal the brokenhearted, to preach deliverance to the captives, and recovering of sight to the blind, to set at liberty them that are bruised, To preach the acceptable year of the Lord. And he closed the book, and he gave it again to the minister, and sat down. And the eyes of all them that were in the synagogue were fastened on him. And he began to say unto them, **This day is this scripture fulfilled in your ears**. Luke 4:14-21

When God, in His unsearchable wisdom, purposed to visit mankind in order to save His creation from sin and death, He sent us His Son, Jesus. The Savior of man spent His life on earth healing the sick, giving sight to the blind, raising the dead, and ultimately laying down His own life as a ransom for many. Every one of the multitudes of those who came to Him found healing, sight, comfort, counsel, truth, and the way of eternal life. How then, was He received by those He came to save? He was:

Rejected

Jesus saith unto them, Did ye never read in the scriptures, The stone which the builders rejected, the same is become the head of the corner: this is the Lord's doing, and it is marvellous in our eyes? Matthew 21:42

Despised

He is despised and rejected of men; a man of sorrows, and acquainted with grief: and we hid as it were our faces from him; he was despised, and we esteemed him not. Isaiah 53:3

Hated

186

If I had not done among them the works which none other man did, they had not had sin: but now have they both seen and hated both me and my Father. John 15:24

Mocked and beaten

And the men that held Jesus mocked him, and smote him. Luke 23:63

Spat upon

And some began to spit on him, and to cover his face, and to buffet him, and to say unto him, Prophesy: and the servants did strike him with the palms of their hands. Mark 14:65

Brutally whipped

Then Pilate therefore took Jesus, and scourged him. John 19:1

Pierced

Behold, he cometh with clouds; and every eye shall see him, and they also which pierced him: and all kindreds of the earth shall wail because of him. Even so, Amen. Revelation 1:7

Murdered by Crucifixion

Ye men of Israel, hear these words; Jesus of Nazareth, a man approved of God among you by miracles and wonders and signs, which God did by him in the midst of you, as ye yourselves also know: Him, being delivered by the determinate counsel and foreknowledge of God, ye have taken, and by wicked hands have crucified and slain: Acts 2:22, 23

Why did this happen? How is it possible that a man who lived a sinless life and performed so many miraculous good deeds could be treated in such a horrific way by those He came to save? What could possibly justify the barbaric acts perpetrated against the Son of God and Prince of Peace? Dear reader, it happened that way to Jesus exactly as He warned it would, and as He warned it would happen to those who follow Him. We have only to look into the Scriptures to find the answers to these questions.

And ye shall be hated of all men for my name's sake: but he that endureth to the end shall be saved. Matthew 10:22

These things I command you, that ye love one another. If the world hate you, ye know that it hated me before it hated you. If ye were of the world, the world would love his own: but because ye are not of the world, but I have chosen you out of the world, therefore the world hateth you. John 15:17-19

He that believeth on him is not condemned: but he that believeth not is condemned already, because he hath not believed in the name of the only begotten Son of God. And this is the condemnation, that light is come into the world, and men loved darkness rather than light, because their deeds were evil. For every one that doeth evil hateth the light, neither cometh to the light, <u>lest his deeds should be reproved</u>. John 3:18-20

Now we get to the heart of the matter and that is exactly what the problem is; a matter of the heart. The heart of man is corrupted by sin. When this truth is revealed to a person, the response is either acceptance or rejection; the latter being far more prevalent, as observed in chapter two when I spoke with the woman who said she was "Spiritual." The truth is a testimony against wickedness. Therefore, the truth must be eradicated by those who reject it because it stands as a condemnation of their way of life.

The heart is deceitful above all things, and desperately wicked: who can know it? Jeremiah 17:9

Is it a wise thing for us to base our lives on what we feel in our hearts? Rather, would it not be wise to listen to the One who formed our ears? Should we not seek He who formed our eyes? Can there be any more critical knowledge to learn than the truth from the One who gave us a mind to know?

Saul was not only on the road to Damascus when he was persecuting believers in Jesus; he was also on the road to damnation. He found the truth and it radically changed his life. He became a faithful follower of the Savior and was driven with a burning desire to get the truth out to as many souls as possible. As the apostle Paul, he dedicated the rest of his life to his Lord and to the many who became believers.

For I have not shunned to declare unto you all the counsel of God. Take heed therefore unto yourselves, and to all the flock, over the which the Holy Ghost hath made you overseers, to feed the church of God, which he hath purchased with his own blood. For I know this, that after my departing shall grievous wolves enter in among you, not sparing the flock. Also of your own selves shall men arise, speaking perverse things, to draw away disciples after them. <u>Therefore watch, and remember, that by the space of three years I ceased not to warn every one night and day with tears.</u> Acts 20:27-31

The most urgent desire in my heart for you dear reader and the first purpose of this book for all who read it, is to proclaim the truth of Jesus Christ to those who have ears to hear. There can be no greater need for any one of us than finding the truth and committing our lives and souls to the only one who can save – Jesus.

Here are some last words from famous Atheists before dying:

Voltaire: "I am abandoned by God and man...I shall go to hell."

Thomas Paine: "I would give worlds, if I had them, that the 'Age of Reason' had never been published. Oh, God, save me; for I am at the edge of hell alone..."

Thomas Carlyle: "I am as good as without hope, a sad old man gazing into the final chasm."

Gandhi: Fifteen years before his death he said, "I must tell you in all humility that Hinduism, as I know it...entirely satisfies my soul, fills my whole being and I find solace in the Bhagavad and the Upanishads." Shortly before his death he wrote, "My days are numbered, I am not likely to live much longer, perhaps a year or more...For the first time in 50 years I find myself in the slough of despond...All about me is darkness; I am praying for light."

Sir Thomas Scott: Chancellor of England. "Until this moment, I thought there was neither God nor Hell...Now I know and feel that there are both, and I am doomed to perdition by the just judgment of the Almighty..."

Edward Gibbon: Author. "All is dark and doubtful."

Mazarin: French cardinal. "Oh, my poor soul! What will become of thee? Whither wilt thou go?"

Thomas Hobbes: Political philosopher and skeptic. "I am about to take a fearful leap into the dark."

Sir Francis Newport: Skeptic. "I know I am lost forever! Oh, that fire! Oh, the insufferable pangs of hell!"

Napoleon Bonaparte: French emperor who brought death to millions to satisfy his greedy, power-mad, selfish ambitions for world conquest: "I die before my time, and my body will be given back to the earth. Such is the fate of him who has been called the great Napoleon. What an abyss between my deep misery and the eternal kingdom of Christ!"

Joseph Stalin: Responsible for the massacre of millions of his own citizens: His deathbed scene as described by his daughter, Svetlana, in Allen Bullock's *Hitler and Stalin.* She says: "The death agony was terrible. God grants an easy death only to the just. He literally choked to death as we watched. At what seemed like the very last moment he suddenly opened his eyes and cast a glance over everyone in the room. It was a terrible glance, insane or perhaps angry and full of fear of death. . .Then something incomprehensible and terrible happened that to this day I can't forget. . .He suddenly lifted his left hand as though he were pointing to something up above and bring down a curse on us all. The gesture was incomprehensible and full of menace. . .The next moment, after a final effort, the spirit wrenched itself free of the flesh."

Let us compare the preceding words with the last words of some well-known believers in Jesus:

Dwight L. Moody: American evangelist and publisher. "Earth recedes. Heaven opens before me. If this is death, it is sweet! There is no valley here. God is calling me, and I must go." Moody's son said, "No, no, Father. You're dreaming." Moody replied, "I am not dreaming. I have been within the gates. This is my triumph; this is my coronation day! It is glorious!"

Joseph Addison: English essayist, poet and politician. "See in what peace a Christian can die."

Thomas à Becket: Archbishop of Canterbury. "I am ready to die for my Lord that in my blood the Church may obtain liberty and peace."

Willielma Campbell: Lady Glen Orchy, Patroness of evangelical missionary work in Scotland and beyond. "If this is dying, it is the pleasantest thing imaginable."

John Bunyan: English Christian writer and preacher, famous for writing The Pilgrim's Progress. "Weep not for me, but for yourselves. The Father of our Lord Jesus Christ, who, through the mediation of His blessed Son, receives me, though a sinner. We shall meet to sing the new song, and remain everlastingly happy."

David Brainerd: Missionary to the American Indians in New York, New Jersey, and eastern Pennsylvania. "I am going into eternity; and it is sweet to me to think of eternity; the endlessness of it makes it sweet. But oh! What shall I say of the future of the wicked! The thought is too dreadful!"

Sir David Brewster: Scottish physicist, mathematician, astronomer, inventor of the kaleidoscope, and writer. "I will see Jesus; I shall see Him as He is! I have had the light for many years. Oh how bright it is! I feel so safe and satisfied!"

Charles Wesley: Anglican priest and co-founder of the Methodist movement, is regarded throughout the world as one of the greatest hymn-writers of all time. He authored over 4,000 published hymns. "I shall be satisfied with Thy likeness. Satisfied!"

Charles Dickens: Author. "I commit my soul to the mercy of God, through our Lord and Saviour Jesus Christ."

Henry Moorhouse: English Evangelist known as the man who moved the man who moved the world. D.L.Moody attributes his power and effectiveness in preaching to the instructions of this one man. During the last years of his life, Henry Moorhouse sold Bibles from a portable carriage. In two years he sold over 150,000 Bibles and gave away millions of books and tracts. "If it were God's will to raise me up [from this sickbed], I should like to preach from the text, John 3:16. Praise be to the Lord."

George Washington: Earnest Christian and the first President of the United States. "Doctor, I am dying, but I am not afraid to die."

Sir Walter Scott: Prolific Scottish historical novelist and poet. "What shall I read?" said Lockhart. "Can you ask?" The dying man replied, "There is only one Book."

William Wilberforce: Member of Parliament, philanthropist and a leader of the movement to abolish the slave trade. "My affections are so much in heaven that I can leave you all without a regret; yet I do not love you less, but God more."

Catherine Booth: Wife of the founder of The Salvation Army, William Booth. "The waters are rising, but so am I. I am not going under, but over. Do not be concerned about dying; go on living well, the dying will be right."

Brownlow North: Bishop of the Church of England. "The blood of Jesus Christ His Son cleanseth us from all sin. That is the verse on which I am now dying. One wants no more."

Thomas Sidney Cooper: English painter member of the Royal Academy of Science in London. "I have full faith in Thy atonement, and I am confident of Thy help. Thy precious blood I fully rely on. Thou art the source of my comfort. I have no other. I want no other."

Field Marshal Frederick Sleigh Roberts: Distinguished Anglo-Irish soldier and one of the most successful commanders of the Victorian era. He died in France while telling those gathered by him of the importance of their studying the Bible: "I ask you to put your trust in God. You will find in this Book guidance when you are in health, comfort when you are in sickness and strength when you are in adversity.'

William Pitt: Earl of Chatham, statesmen, orator, and prime minister. The driving force behind the British victory in the Seven Years War, known as the French and Indian War in North America. "I throw myself on the mercy of God through the merits of Christ."

Henry Wadsworth Longfellow: American educator and poet. "For the Christian, the grave itself is but a covered bridge leading from light to light, through a brief darkness."

Polycarp: (69–155) Disciple of the Apostle John and bishop of the church at Smyrna. "Leave me as I am, the one who gives me strength to endure the fire will also give me strength to stay quite still on the pyre, even without the precaution of your nails.... For eighty and six years I have been his servant, and he has done me no wrong, and how can I blaspheme my King who saved me?"

John Huss: Czech reformist burned by the Roman Catholic Church. When asked at the last moment by the Duke of Bavaria to recant he replied: "What I taught with my lips, I seal with my blood."

John Knox: Scottish clergyman and leader of the Protestant Reformation, considered the founder of the Presbyterian. Bloody Queen Mary once said, she feared the prayers of John Knox more than all of the armies of Scotland. "Live in Christ, and the flesh need not fear death."

Martin Luther: Priest and theology professor who initiated the Protestant Reformation. "Our God is the God from whom cometh salvation. God is the Lord by whom we escape death! Into Thy hands I commit my spirit; God of truth, Thou hast redeemed me!"

Daniel Webster: American statesman, well-known orator and legislator, had William Cowper's hymn read to him: "There is a fountain filled with blood, Drawn from Immanuel's veins." Then he read the last stanza: "Then in a nobler, sweeter song, I'll sing Thy power to save. When this poor lisping, stammering tongue Lies silent in the grave." At this, Webster, one of the most powerful speakers in American history, replied, "Amen! Amen! Amen!"

John Henry Newton: English Anglican clergyman and former slave-ship captain and author of many hymns. Originally a slaver trader, he had a dramatic mid-ocean change of heart that led him to turn his slave ship around and take the people back to their homeland. He became a Presbyterian minister and preached against the slave-trade. He is most famous for having authored the words to the hymn "Amazing Grace." As he neared his end, exclaimed: "I am still in the land of the dying; I shall be in the land of the living soon."

Stephen, (the first martyr of Jesus) upon being stoned to death by his countrymen:

"But he, being full of the Holy Ghost, looked up stedfastly into heaven, and saw the glory of God, and Jesus standing on the right hand of God, And said, Behold, I see the heavens opened, and the Son of man standing on the right hand of God. Acts 7:55, 56

Paul, as his death at the hands of the Romans drew near:

For I am now ready to be offered, and the time of my departure is at hand. I have fought a good fight, I have finished my course, I have kept the faith: Henceforth there is laid up for me a crown of righteousness, which the Lord, the righteous judge, shall give me at that day: and not to me only, but unto all them also that love his appearing. 2 Timothy 4:6-8

What did Jesus say about who it is that loves Him? What does He require of us to prove our love for Him?

He that hath my commandments, and keepeth them, he it is that loveth me: and he that loveth me shall be loved of my Father, and I will love him, and will manifest myself to him. John 14:21

But I say unto you which hear, Love your enemies, do good to them which hate you, Bless them that curse you, and pray for them which despitefully use you. And unto him that smiteth thee on the one cheek offer also the other; and him that taketh away thy cloak forbid not to take thy coat also. Give to every man that asketh of thee; and of him that taketh away thy goods ask them not again. And as ye would that men should do to you, do ye also to them likewise. For if ye love them which love

you, what thank have ye? for sinners also love those that love them. And if ye do good to them which do good to you, what thank have ye? for sinners also do even the same. And if ye lend to them of whom ye hope to receive, what thank have ye? for sinners also lend to sinners, to receive as much again. But <u>love ye your enemies</u>, and do good, and lend, hoping for nothing again; and your reward shall be great, and ye shall be the children of the Highest: for he is kind unto the unthankful and to the evil. <u>Be ye therefore merciful</u>, as your Father also is merciful. <u>Judge not</u>, and ye shall not be judged: condemn not, and ye shall not be condemned: forgive, and ye shall be forgiven: <u>Give</u>, and it shall be given unto you; good measure, pressed down, and shaken together, and running over, shall men give into your bosom. For with the same measure that ye mete withal it shall be measured to you again. Luke 6:27-38

We know that we love Jesus and that He is our Lord by the fruit of our lives as we live in obedience to Him.

And why call ye me, Lord, Lord, and do not the things which I say? Luke 6:46

Every tree that bringeth not forth good fruit is hewn down, and cast into the fire. Wherefore by their fruits ye shall know them. <u>Not every one that saith unto me, Lord, Lord, shall enter into the kingdom of heaven; but he that doeth the will of my Father which is in heaven</u>. Many will say to me in that day, Lord, Lord, have we not prophesied in thy name? and in thy name have cast out devils? and in thy name done many wonderful works? And then will I profess unto them, <u>I never knew you: depart from me, ye that work iniquity</u>. Matthew 7:19-23

We have many great and precious promises from our God, with the gift of eternal life for all who love Him! I would like to close with a few Scriptures that contain the full counsel of God and provide us with tender mercy, loving kindness and the comfort of a God who loves us more than we can even comprehend! This is the truth and the road map to life eternal.

There is therefore now no condemnation to them which are in Christ Jesus, <u>who walk not after the flesh, but after the Spirit</u>. For the law of the Spirit of life in Christ Jesus <u>hath made me free</u> from the law of sin and death. For what the law could not do, in that it was weak through the flesh, <u>God sending his own Son in the likeness of sinful flesh</u>, and for sin, condemned sin in the flesh: That the righteousness of the law might be fulfilled in us, <u>who walk not after the flesh, but after the Spirit</u>. For they that are after the flesh do mind the things of the flesh; but they that are after the Spirit the things of the Spirit. For <u>to be carnally minded is death</u>; but <u>to be spiritually minded is life and peace</u>. Because the carnal mind is enmity against God: for it is not subject to the law of God, neither indeed can be. So then <u>they that are in the flesh cannot please God</u>. But ye are not in the flesh, but in the Spirit, <u>if so be that the Spirit of God dwell in you. Now if any man have not the Spirit of Christ, he is none of his</u>. And if Christ be in you, <u>the body is dead because of sin; but the Spirit is life because of righteousness</u>. But if the Spirit of him that raised up Jesus from the dead dwell in you, he that raised up Christ from the dead <u>shall also quicken your mortal bodies by his Spirit that dwelleth in you</u>. Therefore, brethren, we are debtors, not to the flesh, to live after the flesh. For if ye live after the flesh, <u>ye shall die</u>: but if ye through the Spirit do mortify the deeds of the body, <u>ye shall live. For as many as are led by the Spirit of God, they are the sons of God</u>. For ye have not received the spirit of bondage again to fear; but ye have received the Spirit of adoption, whereby we cry,

Abba, Father. <u>The Spirit itself beareth witness with our spirit,</u> <u>that we are the children of God</u>: And if children, then heirs; heirs of God, and joint-heirs with Christ; if so be that we suffer with him, that we may be also glorified together. For I reckon that the sufferings of this present time are not worthy to be compared with the glory which shall be revealed in us. For the earnest expectation of the creature waiteth for the manifestation of the sons of God. For the creature was made subject to vanity, not willingly, but by reason of him who hath subjected the same in hope, Because the creature itself also shall be delivered from the bondage of corruption into the glorious liberty of the children of God. For we know that the whole creation groaneth and travaileth in pain together until now. And not only they, but ourselves also, which have the firstfruits of the Spirit, even we ourselves groan within ourselves, waiting for the adoption, to wit, the redemption of our body. For we are saved by hope: but hope that is seen is not hope: for what a man seeth, why doth he yet hope for? But if we hope for that we see not, then do we with patience wait for it. Likewise the Spirit also helpeth our infirmities: for we know not what we should pray for as we ought: but the Spirit itself maketh intercession for us with groanings which cannot be uttered. And he that searcheth the hearts knoweth what is the mind of the Spirit, because he maketh intercession for the saints according to the will of God. And we know that <u>all</u> <u>things work together for good to them that love God, to them</u> <u>who are the called according to his purpose</u>. For whom he did foreknow, he also did predestinate to be conformed to the image of his Son, that he might be the firstborn among many brethren. Moreover whom he did predestinate, them he also called: and whom he called, them he also justified: and whom he justified, them he also glorified. What shall we then say to these things? <u>If God be for us, who can be against us</u>? He that spared not his own Son, but delivered him up for us all, how shall he not with him also freely give us all things? Who shall lay any thing to the charge of God's elect? It is God that justifieth. Who is he that condemneth? It is Christ that died, yea rather, that is risen again, who is even at the right hand of God, who also maketh intercession for us. Who shall separate us from the love of Christ? shall tribulation, or distress, or persecution, or famine, or nakedness, or peril, or sword? As it is written, For thy sake we are killed all the day long; we are accounted as sheep for the slaughter. Nay, in all these things we are more than conquerors through him that loved us. For I am persuaded, that neither death, nor life, nor angels, nor principalities, nor powers, nor things present, nor things to come, Nor height, nor depth, nor any other creature, shall be able to separate us from the love of God, which is in Christ Jesus our Lord. Romans 8

Would you meditate on the following prayer that Jesus prayed for you while He was in the world and soon to be put to death for you sins, so that you might have life?

These words spake Jesus, and lifted up his eyes to heaven, and said, Father, the hour is come; glorify thy Son, that thy Son also may glorify thee: As thou hast given him power over all flesh, that he should give eternal life to as many as thou hast given him. And this is life eternal, that they might know thee the only true God, and Jesus Christ, whom thou hast sent. I have glorified thee on the earth: I have finished the work which thou gavest me to do. And now, O Father, glorify thou me with thine own self with the glory which I had with thee before the world was. I have manifested thy name unto the men which thou gavest me out of the world: thine they were, and thou gavest them me; and they have kept thy word. Now they have known that all things whatsoever thou hast given me are of thee. For I have given unto them the words which thou gavest me; and they have received them, and have known surely that I came out from thee, and they have believed that thou didst send me. I pray for them: I pray not for the world, but for them which thou hast given me; for they are thine. And all mine are thine, and thine are mine; and I am glorified in them. And now I am no more in the world, but these are in the world, and I come to thee. Holy Father, keep through thine own name those whom thou hast given me, that they may be one, as we are. While I was with them in the world, I kept them in thy name: those that thou gavest me I have kept, and none of them is lost, but the son of perdition; that the scripture might be fulfilled. And now come I to thee; and these things I speak in the world, that they might have my joy fulfilled in themselves. I have given them thy word; and the world hath hated them, because they are not of the world, even as I am not of the world. I pray not that thou shouldest take them out of the world, but that thou shouldest keep them from the evil. They are not of the world, even as I am not of the world. Sanctify them through thy truth: thy word is truth. As thou hast sent me into the world, even so have I also sent them into the world. And for their sakes I sanctify myself, that they also might be sanctified through the truth. Neither pray I for these alone, but for them also which shall believe on me through their word; That they all may be one; as thou, Father, art in me, and I in thee, that they also may be one in us: that the world may believe that thou hast sent me. And the glory which thou gavest me I have given them; that they may be one, even as we are one: I in them, and thou in me, that they may be made perfect in one; and that the world may know that thou hast sent me, and hast loved them, as thou hast loved me. Father, I will that they also, whom thou hast given me, be with me where I am; that they may behold my glory, which thou hast given me: for thou lovedst me before the foundation of the world. O righteous Father, the world hath not known thee: but

201

I have known thee, and these have known that thou hast sent
me. And I have declared unto them thy name, and will declare
it: that the love wherewith thou hast loved me may be in them,
and I in them. John 17

-Jesus

Chapter 10

THE ORIGINAL GOSPEL

Jesus answered and said unto him, Verily, verily, I say unto thee, Except a man be born again, he cannot see the kingdom of God.
John 3:3

My purpose in writing this book is to present the true gospel of Jesus Christ. What is the original gospel? How do I apply it in my life? How do I become a Christian? Is there any hope for me if I used to be and I have fallen away from the faith? What does it really meant to be a Christian? Is it worth it? What will I lose if do become one? What will I gain?

Oswald Chambers had this to say regarding the truth:

"In the teachings of Jesus Christ the element of judgment is always brought out – it is the sign of the love of God. Never sympathize with someone who finds it difficult to get to God; God is not to blame. It is not for us to figure out the reason for the difficulty, but only to present the truth of God so that the Spirit of God will reveal what is wrong. The greatest test of the quality of our preaching is whether or not it brings everyone to judgment. When the truth is preached, the Spirit of God brings each person face to face with God Himself." Oswald Chamber, *My Utmost for His Highest.*

Let us start by defining some terms:

Gospel

The good or joyful message of the birth, life, actions, death, resurrection, ascension and doctrines of Jesus Christ; a revelation of the grace of God to fallen man through a mediator, including the character, actions, and doctrines of Christ, with the whole scheme of salvation, as revealed by Christ and his apostles. This gospel is said to have been preached to Abraham, by the promise, "in thee shall all nations be blessed."

Repentance

Sorrow for anything done or said; the pain or grief which a person experiences in consequence of the injury or inconvenience produced by his own conduct; the pain, regret or affliction that a person feels as a consequence of his or her past conduct. Real penitence is a sorrow or deep contrition for sin, as an offense and dishonor to God, a violation of his holy law, and the basest ingratitude towards a Being of infinite benevolence. This is called evangelical repentance, and is accompanied and followed by amendment of life. Repentance is a change of mind, or a conversion from sin to God. Repentance is the relinquishment of any practice, from conviction that it has offended God. Godly sorrow worketh repentance to salvation (2 Cor. 7; Mat. 3).

Believe

To credit upon the authority or testimony of another; to be persuaded of the truth of something upon the declaration of another, or upon evidence furnished by reasons, arguments, and deductions of the mind, or by other circumstances, than personal knowledge. When we believe upon the authority of another, we always put confidence in his veracity; to expect or hope with confidence; to trust. To believe in, is to hold as the object of faith.

204

"Ye believe in God, believe also in me." (John 14). To believe on, is to trust, to place full confidence in, to rest upon with faith. "To them gave he power to become the sons of God, even to them that believe on his name." (John 1). If we truly believe, our faith will be manifested by a visibly changed life.

Born Again

To be born again is to be regenerated and renewed; to receive spiritual life (John 3).

One of the leaders of Israel was so vexed by the teachings of Jesus regarding the concept of being born again, that He actually approached Jesus at night to learn the truth.

There was a man of the Pharisees, named Nicodemus, a ruler of the Jews: The same came to Jesus by night, and said unto him, Rabbi, we know that thou art a teacher come from God: for no man can do these miracles that thou doest, except God be with him. Jesus answered and said unto him, <u>Verily, verily, I say unto thee, Except a man be born again, he cannot see the kingdom of God</u>. Nicodemus saith unto him, How can a man be born when he is old? can he enter the second time into his mother's womb, and be born? Jesus answered, Verily, verily, I say unto thee, Except a man be born of water and of the Spirit, he cannot enter into the kingdom of God. That which is born of the flesh is flesh; and <u>that which is born of the Spirit is spirit</u>. Marvel not that I said unto thee, Ye must be born again. The wind bloweth where it listeth (inclines or leans), **and thou hearest the sound thereof, but canst not tell whence it cometh, and whither it goeth: <u>so is every one that is born of the Spirit</u>. Nicodemus answered and said unto him, How can these things be? Jesus answered and said unto him, Art thou a master of Israel, and knowest not these things? Verily, verily, I say unto**

thee, We speak that we do know, and testify that we have seen; and ye receive not our witness. If I have told you earthly things, and ye believe not, how shall ye believe, if I tell you of heavenly things? And no man hath ascended up to heaven, but he that came down from heaven, even the Son of man which is in heaven. And as Moses lifted up the serpent in the wilderness, even so must the Son of man be lifted up: That whosoever believeth in him should not perish, but have eternal life. For God so loved the world, that he gave his only begotten Son, that whosoever believeth in him should not perish, but have everlasting life. For God sent not his Son into the world to condemn the world; but that the world through him might be saved. **He that believeth on him is not condemned: but he that believeth not is condemned already, because he hath not believed in the name of the only begotten Son of God. And this is the condemnation, that light is come into the world, and men loved darkness rather than light, because their deeds were evil. For every one that doeth evil hateth the light, neither cometh to the light, lest his deeds should be reproved. But he that doeth truth cometh to the light, that his deeds may be made manifest, that they are wrought in God.** John 3:1-21

We all were born once into the world of mankind through the flesh. In order to be adopted into the family of God, we must be born again. Before this occurs, the first thing any of us must realize is that we have transgressed against God. There is no getting around that. The truth is that we are ALL children of disobedience and subject to the wrath of God for our sin. In our world today, there are _many_ cults, religions, philosophies, doctrines, ideas, and so-called spiritual leaders who teach that there is no such thing as sin and therefore no need for a "Savior." Not surprisingly, many also hold that there is no hell, no devil, and no judgment to come. These errors are overwhelmingly accepted by the majority, because such beliefs do not condemn our actions, nor do they require us to change the way we live our lives. That is why the cross is offensive to most and rejected by the same as well.

For Christ sent me not to baptize, but to preach the gospel: not with wisdom of words, lest the cross of Christ should be made of none effect. <u>For the preaching of the cross is to them that perish foolishness; but unto us which are saved it is the power of God</u>. For it is written, I will destroy the wisdom of the wise, and will bring to nothing the understanding of the prudent. 1 Corinthians 1:17-19

What is the truth?

But now the righteousness of God without the law is manifested, being witnessed by the law and the prophets; Even the righteousness of God which is by faith of Jesus Christ unto all and upon all them that believe: for there is no difference: <u>For all have sinned, and come short of the glory of God</u>; Being justified freely by his grace through the redemption that is in Christ Jesus: Whom God hath set forth to be a propitiation through faith in his blood, to declare his righteousness <u>for the remission of sins that are past</u>, through the forbearance of God; To declare, I say, at this time his righteousness: that he might be just, and the justifier of him which believeth in Jesus. Romans 3:21-26

So, what are we to do? Many others have asked the same question.

And the keeper of the prison awaking out of his sleep, and seeing the prison doors open, he drew out his sword, and would have killed himself, supposing that the prisoners had been fled. But Paul cried with a loud voice, saying, Do thyself no harm: for we are all here. Then he called for a light, and sprang in,

and came trembling, and fell down before Paul and Silas, And brought them out, and said, Sirs, <u>what must I do to be saved</u>? And they said, Believe on the Lord Jesus Christ, and thou shalt be saved, and thy house. And they spake unto him the word of the Lord, and to all that were in his house. And he took them the same hour of the night, and washed their stripes; and was baptized, he and all his, straightway. And when he had brought them into his house, he set meat before them, and rejoiced, believing in God with all his house. Acts 16:27-34

Salvation brings about a radical lifestyle change, as can be seen in the actions of Paul's jailer. Proof of our repentance is evidenced by a changed life.

For as many as are led by the Spirit of God, they are the sons of God. For ye have not received the spirit of bondage again to fear; but ye have received <u>the Spirit of adoption, whereby we cry, Abba, Father</u>. The Spirit itself beareth witness with our spirit, that we are the children of God: Romans 8:14-16

When we hear the gospel of Jesus Christ, faith is made alive and we can be born again.

That if thou shalt confess with thy mouth the Lord Jesus, and shalt believe in thine heart that God hath raised him from the dead, thou shalt be saved. Romans 10:9

You have learned the truth. What you do with it is up to you.

So then faith cometh by hearing, and hearing by the word of God. Romans 10:17

If you do not know Jesus, or walked away from Him in the past, I am pleading with you to call on Him, seek Him, return to Him, surrender your life to Him and obey Him. It all starts with you, dear reader. There can be no other matter important in your life, than making peace with God.

Therefore being justified by faith, we have peace with God through our Lord Jesus Christ: By whom also we have access by faith into this grace wherein we stand, and rejoice in hope of the glory of God. Romans 5:1, 2

I hope that this book has blessed you and my prayer for every reader is that God will make the truth of His Son Jesus known to your heart, and that you will make Him your Lord and Savior.

And, behold, I come quickly; and my reward is with me, to give every man according as his work shall be. I am Alpha and Omega, the beginning and the end, the first and the last. Blessed are they that do his commandments, that they may have right to the tree of life, and may enter in through the gates into the city. Revelation 22:12-14

Epilogue

If you have made a commitment to Jesus, you have made a wise choice. You have been adopted into the family of God and are now my brother or sister! I praise our Father for you, dear reader! The next steps are critical to the well-being of your soul as your faith in Christ grows. The enemy of all souls uses the same tactics that have worked for him throughout history to defeat new believers. You can expect the following in your life:

- People who are close to you and that you respect will come against you regarding your new faith. Remember, a prophet has no honor in his own house. They will be watching you for any misstep or mistake. Just keep your focus above on Jesus and seek Him daily with all your heart (John 15).
- You will feel pressure from others that you used to associate with. Remember the words of Jesus when He said if they hate you, they hated me first (John 15:18). In your old life, you were going down river and on the broad road that leads to destruction. Now that you have turned up river, you will feel the pressure of the current against you. Do not give up. Greater is He that is in you than He that is in the world (1 John 4:4).
- You now have four enemies who are dead set against your heart's desire to follow Jesus: the world, the devil, your mind, and your flesh. It is now a spiritual battle and you must put on the full armor of God every day, or you will be defeated. Find out what that armor is and wear it daily (Eph. 6:10-17).
- We all have sinned and we all stumble, beloved brother and beloved sister. Do not despair and do not try to hide your sins. Confess them to your Father and he will forgive you

all unrighteousness (1 John 1:9). Forget what is past and run the race marked out for you (Phil. 3:13-15).

- Don't ever look back or be tempted to go back to your old life; ever! Remember Lot's wife (Luke 17:32).

Beloved saint, make every effort to diligently do this:

- Each morning, go to your own "Secret place" (anywhere that is private) and pray to your Heavenly Father in the name of Jesus. Thank Him and praise Him for His many tender mercies and loving kindnesses toward you (Psalm 100).
- Talk to your heavenly Father and ask Him in the name of Jesus to fill you with His Holy Spirit. Thank Him for everything. Ask, and it shall be given you; seek, and you shall find; knock, and it shall be opened unto you. For every one that asks receives, and he that seeks finds, and to him that knocks it shall be opened (Luke 11:9, 10).
- Read your Bible daily, preferable at the start of your day, every day, at the same time and in a quiet place if possible. Jesus is the bread of life and whoever comes to Him shall never hunger, and he that believes on Him shall never thirst (John 6:34-36).
- Pray to the Father that He will bring other earnest believers into your life for fellowship, comfort, edification, and encouragement to do good works in the Lord. (Heb. 10:25).
- Make every effort to add to your faith; virtue, knowledge, temperance, patience, godliness, brotherly kindness and charity (1 Peter 1:5-7).
- Think on good things (Philippians 4:8).
- Avoid what is profane that the world follows after. Friendship with the world is enmity with God (James 4:4).

- Be careful to work out your own salvation with fear and trembling (Philippians 2:12).
- Abide in Jesus each day for the rest of your life (John 15).

Recommended Reading:

1. Abide in Christ by Andrew Murray
2. Holiness by J.C. Ryle
3. I Die Daily by Todd Tomasella*
4. My Utmost for His Highest by Oswald Chambers
5. More Than a Carpenter by Josh Mcdowell
6. Pilgrim's Progress by John Bunyan
7. Predators in the Pulpit by Todd Tomasella*
8. The Case for Christ by Lee Strobel
9. The Cost of Discipleship by Dietrich Bonhoeffer
10. Lie of the Ages by Todd Tomasella*
11. The Person and Work of the Holy Spirit by R.A. Torrey

*these books are available at www.safeguardyoursoul.com

Lamplighter Publishing

But when he saw the multitudes, he was moved with compassion on them, because they fainted, and were scattered abroad, as sheep having no shepherd. Then saith he unto his disciples, The harvest truly is plenteous, but the labourers are few; Pray ye therefore the Lord of the harvest, that he will send forth labourers into his harvest. Matthew 9:36-38

Jesus

41772310R00122

Made in the USA
Charleston, SC
08 May 2015